ESTATE PUB

OXFORDSHIRE

Street Maps of 41 Towns
with index to streets
Road Map with index
Administrative Districts Map
Population Gazetteer

Street plans prepared and published by ESTATE PUBLICATIONS, and based upon the ORDNANCE SURVEY maps with the sanction of the controller of H.M. Stationery Office.   Crown Copyright reserved

The publishers acknowledge the co-operation of the local authorities of towns represented in this atlas.

ISBN 0 86084 400 5

ESTATE PUBLICATIONS

STREET ATLASES

ASHFORD, TENTERDEN
BASILDON, BRENTWOOD
BASINGSTOKE, ANDOVER
BOURNEMOUTH, POOLE, CHRISTCHURCH
BRIGHTON, LEWES, NEWHAVEN, SEAFORD
BROMLEY (London Borough),
CHELMSFORD, BRAINTREE, MALDON, WITHAM
CHICHESTER, BOGNOR REGIS
COLCHESTER, CLACTON
CRAWLEY & MID SUSSEX
DERBY, HEANOR, CASTLE DONNINGTON
EDINBURGH
EXETER, EXMOUTH
FAREHAM, GOSPORT
FOLKESTONE, DOVER, DEAL
GLOUCESTER, CHELTENHAM
GRAVESEND, DARTFORD
GUILDFORD, WOKING
HASTINGS, EASTBOURNE, HAILSHAM
HIGH WYCOMBE
I. OF WIGHT TOWNS
LEICESTER
MAIDSTONE
MANSFIELD
MEDWAY, GILLINGHAM
NEW FOREST
NOTTINGHAM, EASTWOOD, HUCKNALL, ILKESTON
OXFORD
PLYMOUTH, IVYBRIDGE, SALTASH, TORPOINT
PORTSMOUTH, HAVANT
READING
REIGATE, BANSTEAD, REDHILL
RYE & ROMNEY MARSH
ST. ALBANS, WELWYN, HATFIELD
SALISBURY, AMESBURY, WILTON
SEVENOAKS
SHREWSBURY
SLOUGH, MAIDENHEAD
SOUTHAMPTON, EASTLEIGH
SOUTHEND-ON-SEA
SWALE (Sittingbourne, Faversham, I. of Sheppey)
SWINDON
TELFORD
THANET, CANTERBURY, HERNE BAY, WHITSTABLE
TORBAY
TUNBRIDGE WELLS, TONBRIDGE, CROWBOROUGH
WATFORD, HEMEL HEMPSTEAD
WINCHESTER, NEW ALRESFORD
WORTHING, LITTLEHAMPTON, ARUNDEL

COUNTY ATLASES

AVON
AVON & SOMERSET
BERKSHIRE
CHESHIRE
CORNWALL
DEVON
DORSET
ESSEX
HAMPSHIRE
HERTFORDSHIRE
KENT (64pp)
KENT (128pp)
OXFORDSHIRE
SHROPSHIRE
SOMERSET
SURREY
SUSSEX (64pp)
SUSSEX (128pp)
WILTSHIRE

LEISURE MAPS

SOUTH EAST (1:200,000)
KENT & EAST SUSSEX (1:150,000)
SURREY & SUSSEX (1:150,000)
SOUTHERN ENGLAND (1:200,000)
ISLE OF WIGHT (1:50,000)
WESSEX (1:200,000)
DEVON & CORNWALL (1:200,000)
CORNWALL (1:180,000)
DEVON (1:200,000)
DARTMOOR & SOUTH DEVON COAST (1:100,000)
GREATER LONDON (1:80,000)
EAST ANGLIA (1:250,000)
THAMES & CHILTERNS (1:200,000)
COTSWOLDS & WYEDEAN (1:200,000)
HEART OF ENGLAND (1:250,000)
WALES (1:250,000)
THE SHIRES OF MIDDLE ENGLAND (1:250,000)
SHROPSHIRE, STAFFORDSHIRE (1:200,000)
SNOWDONIA (1:125,000)
YORKSHIRE & HUMBERSIDE (1:250,000)
YORKSHIRE DALES (1:125,000)
NORTH YORK MOORS (1:125,000)
NORTH WEST ENGLAND (1:200,000)
ISLE OF MAN (1:60,000)
NORTH PENNINES & LAKES (1:200,000)
LAKE DISTRICT (1:75,000)
BORDERS OF ENGLAND & SCOTLAND (1:200,000)
BURNS COUNTRY (1:200,000)
ISLE OF ARRAN (1:63,360)
ARGYLL & THE ISLES (1:200,000)
HEART OF SCOTLAND (1:200,000)
GREATER GLASGOW (1:150,000)
LOCH LOMOND & TROSSACHS (1:150,000)
PERTHSHIRE (1:150,000)
FORT WILLIAM, BEN NEVIS, GLEN COE (1:185,000)
IONA (1:10,000) & MULL (1:115,000)
GRAMPIAN HIGHLANDS (1:185,000)
LOCH NESS & INVERNESS (1:150,000)
AVIEMORE & SPEY VALLEY (1:150,000)
SKYE & LOCHALSH (1:130,000)
CAITHNESS & SUTHERLAND (1:185,000)
WESTERN ISLES (1:125,000)
ORKNEY & SHETLAND (1:128,000)
ENGLAND & WALES (1:650,000)
SCOTLAND (1:500,000)
GREAT BRITAIN (1:1,100,000)

ROAD ATLAS

MOTORING IN THE SOUTH (1:200,000)

EUROPEAN LEISURE MAPS

EUROPE (1:3,100,000)
BENELUX (1:600,000)
FRANCE (1:1,000,000)
GERMANY (1:1,000,000)
GREECE & THE AEGEAN (1:1,000,000)
IRELAND (1:625,000)
ITALY (1:1,000,000)
MEDITERRANEAN CRUISING (1:5,000,000)
SCANDINAVEA (1:2,600,000)
SPAIN & PORTUGAL (1:1,000,000)
THE ALPS (1:1,000,000)
THE WORLD (1:35,000,000)
THE WORLD FLAT SHEET

ESTATE PUBLICATIONS are also
sole distributors in the U.K. for:
ORDNANCE SURVEY, Republic of Ireland
ORDNANCE SURVEY, Northern Ireland

CONTENTS

Scale of street plans: 4 inches to 1 mile (unless otherwise stated on map).

One-way street	→	Post Office	●
Pedestrianized	▨▨▨	Public Convenience	Ⓒ
Car Park	Ⓟ	Place of worship	✚

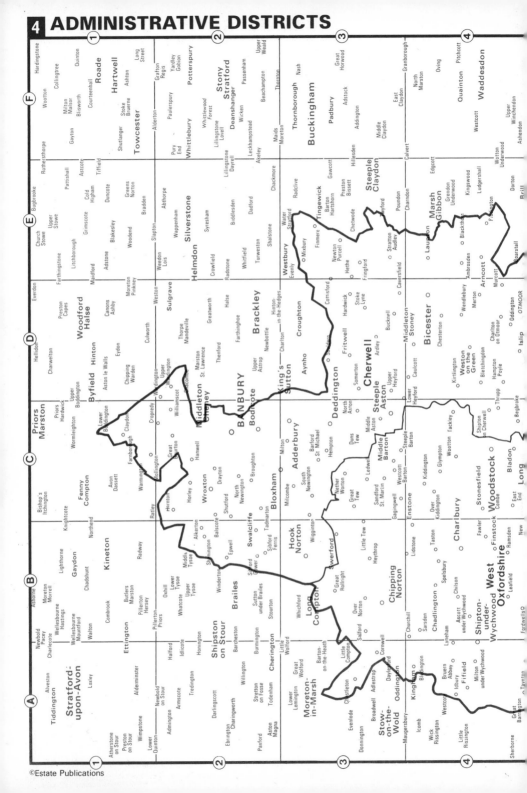

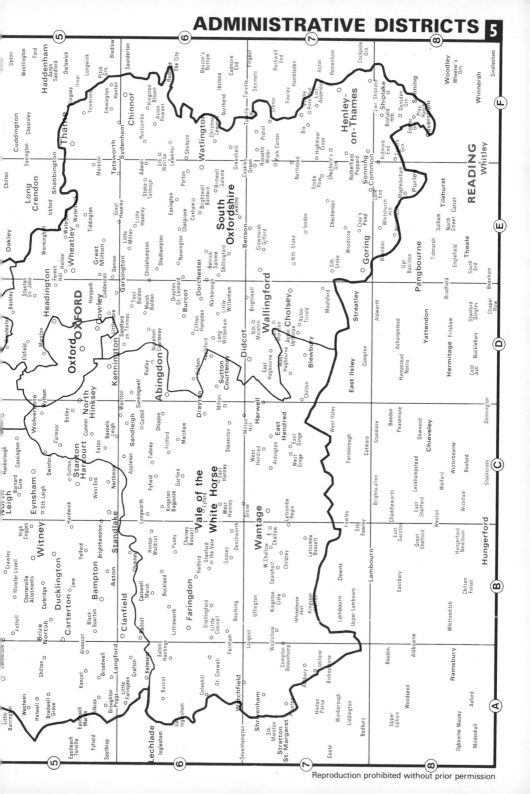

GAZETTEER INDEX TO ROAD MAP
With populations

County of Oxfordshire population **519,490**

Districts:
Cherwell **107,759**
Oxford **99,195**
South Oxford **129,624**
Vale of White Horse **101,825**
West Oxfordshire **81,087**

Abingdon **22,862**	11 E3
Adderbury **2,417**	8 D3
Adwell **24**	11 G3
Alkerton (with Shenington) **360**	8 C2
Alvescot **337**	10 B2
Ambrosden **1,257**	9 F5
Appleford **398**	11 E4
Appleton (with Eaton) **837**	10 D3
Ardington **287**	10 D4
Ardley **692**	9 E4
Arncott **978**	9 F5
Ascott under Wychwood **488**	8 B5
Ashbury **527**	10 B5
Asthall **234**	8 B6
Asthall Leigh	8 B6
Aston, Bampton & Shifford **681**	10 C3
Aston Rowant **826**	11 G3
Aston Tirrold **364**	11 E5
Aston Upthorpe **178**	11 E5
Balscote	8 C2
Bampton **1,973**	10 B2
Banbury **36,086**	8 D2
Barford St Michael & St John **552**	8 D3
Barnard Gate	8 C6
Baulking **101**	10 B4
Beckley **611**	9 E6
Begbroke **755**	8 D6
Benson **4,030**	11 F4
Berrick Salome **2,991**	11 F4
Bessels Leigh **83**	10 D3
Bicester **14,492**	9 E5
Binfield Heath	11 H6
Bix **669**	11 G5
Black Bourton & Carterton **11,277**	10 B2
Blackthorn **661**	9 F5
Bladon **739**	8 D6
Blenheim **125**	*
Bletchingdon **822**	9 E5
Blewbury **1,475**	11 E5
Bloxham **2,653**	8 D3
Bodicote **2,105**	8 D3
Botley	10 D2
Bourton **272**	10 A4
Bourton **599**	*
Bradwell Grove	10 A2
Brighthampton	10 C2
Brightwell (cum Sotwell) **1,487**	11 F4
Brightwell Baldwin **176**	11 G4
Britwell Salome **168**	11 G4
Brize Norton **849**	10 B2
Broadwell **132**	10 A2
Broughton **336**	8 D3
Broughton Poggs & Filkins **374**	10 A3
Bruern Abbey **74**	8 B5
Buckland **511**	10 C3
Bucknell **292**	9 E4
Burcot	11 E3
Burford **1,371**	8 A6
Buscot **181**	10 A3

Cane End	11 G6
Carswell Marsh	10 B3
Carterton & Black Bourton **11,277**	10 B2
Cassington **662**	8 D6
Caulcott	9 E5
Caversfield **568**	9 F4
Chadlington **749**	8 B5
Chalgrove **2,527**	11 F3
Charlbury **2,643**	8 C5
Charlton on Otmoor **377**	9 E6
Charney Bassett **254**	10 C4
Charterville Allotments	8 B6
Chastleton **109**	8 A4
Checkendon **1,030**	11 G5
Chesterton **1,120**	9 E5
Childrey **443**	10 C5
Chilson **109**	8 B5
Chilton **966**	10 D5
Chimney	10 C3
Chinnor **5,988**	11 H3
Chipping Norton **5,114**	8 B4
Chislehampton	11 F3
Cholsey **3,905**	11 F5
Christmas Common	11 G4
Church Hanborough	8 D6
Churchill **440**	8 B4
Clanfield **822**	10 B3
Claydon (with Clattercot) **328**	8 D1
Clifton Hampden **631**	11 E4
Coleshill **164**	10 A4
Combe **657**	8 C6
Compton Beauchamp **66**	10 B5
Cookley Green	11 G4
Cornbury & Wychwood **71**	*
Cornwell **70**	8 B4
Cothill	10 D3
Cottisford **167**	9 F4
Cowley	11 E2
Crawley **143**	8 C6
Cray's Pond	11 F6
Cropedy **665**	8 D1
Crowell **106**	*
Crowmarsh Gifford **1,398**	11 F4
Cuddesdon & Denton **432**	11 F2
Culham **436**	11 E4
Cumnor **4,234**	10 D2
Curbridge **418**	10 B2
Cuxham (with Easington) **160**	11 G4
Deddington **1,617**	8 D4
Denchworth **156**	10 C4
Denton & Cuddesdon **432**	11 F3
Didcot **14,143**	11 E4
Dorchester **1,045**	11 F4
Drayton **247**	8 D2
Drayton **2,039**	10 D4
Drayton St Leonard **274**	11 F3
Ducklington **1,237**	10 C2
Duns Tew **247**	8 D4
Dunsden Green & Eye **526**	11 H6
Easington (with Cuxham) **160**	11 G3
East Challow **1,317**	10 C4
East End	8 C6
East Ginge	10 D5
East Hagbourne **1,061**	11 E4
East Hanney **775**	10 D4
East Hendred **1,114**	10 D5
Eaton (with Appleton) **837**	10 D2
Eaton Hastings **82**	10 B3
Elsfield **82**	9 E6

Enstone **1,022**	8 C4
Epwell **222**	8 C2
Ewelme **933**	11 F4
Emmer Green	11 G6
Eynsham **4,449**	10 D2
Faringdon **4,672**	10 B4
Farmoor	10 D2
Fawler **120**	8 C5
Fencott & Murcott **158**	9 F6
Fernham **195**	10 B4
Fifield **120**	8 A5
Filkins & Broughton Poggs **374**	10 A2
Finmere **371**	9 F3
Finstock **726**	8 C6
Fordwells	8 B6
Forest Hill (with Shotover) **624**	11 F2
Freeland **1,374**	8 C6
Frilford **196**	10 D3
Fringford **403**	9 F4
Fritwell **403**	9 E4
Fulbrook **338**	8 B6
Fyfield & Tubney **506**	10 D3
Gagingwell	8 C4
Garford **128**	10 D3
Garsington **1,784**	11 F3
Glympton **120**	8 D5
Godington **45**	*
Goosey **130**	10 C4
Goring **3,465**	11 F6
Goring Heath **1,285**	*
Gosford & Water Eaton **1,782**	*
Grafton & Radcot **39**	10 B3
Great Bourton	8 D2
Great Coxwell **317**	10 B4
Great Haseley **589**	11 F3
Great Milton **812**	11 F2
Great Rollright **525**	8 B4
Great Tew **157**	8 C4
Greenfield	11 G4
Grove **7,457**	10 C4
Hailey **1,100**	8 C6
Hampton Poyle & Gay **152**	9 E6
Hanwell **184**	8 D2
Hardwick (with Tusmore) **70**	9 F4
Hardwick (with Yelford) **103**	10 C2
Harpsden **501**	*
Harwell **2,275**	10 D4
Hatford **102**	10 C4
Headington	11 E2
Hempton	8 D4
Henley-on-Thames **11,180**	11 H5
Hensington Without **1,106**	*
Hethe **283**	9 F4
Heythrop **122**	8 C4
High Cogges	8 C6
Highmoor Cross **355**	11 G5
Hinton Waldrist **282**	10 C3
Holton **368**	11 F2
Holwell **22**	10 A2
Hook Norton **1,649**	8 C3
Horley **260**	8 C2
Hornton **310**	8 C2
Horspath **1,632**	11 F2
Horton-cum-Studley **500**	9 F6
Idbury **113**	8 A5
Idstone	10 B5
Ipsden **329**	11 F5
Islip **670**	9 E6

Place	Population	Map ref
Kelmscot	85	10 A3
Kencot	111	10 A2
Kennington	4,135	11 E3
Kiddington (with Asterleigh)	123	8 D5
Kidlington	12,626	9 E6
Kidmore End	1,427	11 G6
Kingham	576	8 A5
Kingston Bagpuize (with Southmoor)	1,823	10 C3
Kingston Blount		11 H3
Kingston Lisle	256	10 B5
Kirtlington	836	9 E5
Langford	293	10 B5
Launton	1,309	9 F5
Leafield	735	8 B6
Ledwell		8 D4
Letcombe Bassett	186	10 C5
Letcombe Regis	521	10 C5
Lew	408	10 B2
Lewknor	434	11 G3
Lidstone		8 C5
Little Coxwell	134	10 B4
Little Faringdon	67	10 A3
Little Haseley		11 F3
Little Milton		11 F3
Little Tew	172	8 C4
Little Wittenham	66	11 E4
Littlemore	7,953	11 E3
Littleworth	191	10 B3
Lockinge	174	*
Long Hanborough		8 D6
Long Wittenham	891	11 E4
Longcot	424	10 B4
Longworth	680	10 C3
Lower Heyford	435	8 D4
Lower Shiplake		11 H6
Lyford	48	10 C4
Lyneham	144	8 B5
Mapledurham	320	11 G6
Marcham	1,676	10 D3
Marsh Baldon	290	11 E3
Marston	3,494	11 E2
Merton	451	9 F5
Middle Aston	108	8 D4
Middle Barton		8 D4
Middleton Stoney	238	9 E4
Milcombe	614	8 C3
Milton	190	8 D3
Milton	760	10 D4
Milton under Wychwood	1,501	8 B5
Milton Hill		10 D4
Minster Lovell	1,364	8 B6
Mixbury	212	9 F3
Mollington	380	8 D1
Moreton		11 G2
Moulsford	494	11 F5
Murcott & Fencott	158	9 F6
Nether Worton		8 D4
Nettlebed	681	11 G5
New Yatt		8 C6
Newington	132	11 F3
Newton Purcell (with Shelswell)	62	9 F4
Noke	97	9 E6
North Aston	209	8 D4
North Hinksey	4,053	10 D2
North Leigh	1,859	8 C6
North Moreton	317	11 E4
North Newington	273	8 C2
North Stoke		11 F5
Northmoor	366	10 D3
Nuffield	573	*
Nuneham Courtney	177	11 E3
Oddington	75	9 E6
Over Kiddington		8 C5
Over Norton	461	8 B4
Oxford	99,195	11 E2
Park Corner		11 G5
Piddington	290	9 F5
Pishill (with Stonor)	292	11 G4
Play Hatch		11 H6
Postcombe		11 G3
Prescote	14	*
Purley		11 G6
Pusey	54	10 C3
Pyrton	241	11 G3
Radcot & Grafton	39	10 B3
Radley	3,691	11 E3
Ramsden	385	8 C6
Risinghurst & Sandhills	2,985	*
Rotherfield Greys	335	*
Rotherfield Peppard	1,388	11 G5
Rousham	58	*
Russells Water		11 G4
St Helen Without	3,183	*
Salford	318	8 B4
Sandford on Thames	655	11 E3
Sandford St Martin	198	8 C4
Sandleigh		10 D3
Sarsden	82	8 B5
Shellingford	171	10 B4
Shenington (with Alkerton)	360	8 C2
Shepherd's Green		11 G5
Shillingford		11 F4
Shilton	461	10 B2
Shiplake	2,034	11 H6
Shippon		10 D3
Shipton on Cherwell & Thrupp	362	8 D5
Shipton-under-Wychwood	1,120	8 B5
Shirburn	109	11 G3
Shrivenham	2,273	10 A4
Shutford	289	8 C2
Sibford Ferris	302	8 C3
Sibford Gower	456	8 C3
Somerton	204	9 E4
Sonning Common	3,763	11 G6
Souldern	389	9 E4
South Hinksey	338	*
South Leigh	400	10 C2
South Moreton	340	11 E4
South Newington	291	8 C3
South Stoke	548	11 F5
South Weston		11 G3
Sparsholt	288	10 C5
Spelsbury	293	8 C5
Stadhampton	706	11 F3
Standlake	1,289	10 C3
Stanford in the Vale	1,565	10 C4
Stanton Harcourt	774	10 D2
Stanton St John	428	9 F6
Steeple Aston	874	8 D4
Steeple Barton	1,354	8 D4
Steventon	1,376	10 D4
Stoke Lyne	220	9 E4
Stoke Row	644	11 G5
Stoke Talmage	55	11 G3
Stonesfield	1,370	8 C5
Stratton Audley	309	9 F4
Sunningwell	1,170	10 D3
Sutton		10 D2
Sutton Courtenay	2,337	11 E4
Swalcliffe	175	8 C3
Swerford	123	8 C4
Swinbrook & Widford	157	8 B6
Swinford		10 D2
Swyncombe	270	*
Sydenham	339	11 G3
Tackley	816	8 D5
Tadmarton	406	8 C3
Taston		8 C5
Taynton	82	8 A6
Tetsworth	509	11 G3
Thame	9,022	11 G2
Thomley	7	*
Thrupp		8 D6
Tiddington (with Albury)	573	11 F2
Tokers Green		11 G6
Toot Baldon	168	11 E3
Towersey	434	11 H2
Tubney & Fyfield	506	10 D3
Uffington	731	10 B4
Upper Heyford	2,381	9 E4
Upper Wardington		9 E2
Upton	406	*
Wallingford	6,374	11 F4
Wantage	8,899	10 C4
Warborough	1,012	11 F4
Wardington	541	9 E1
Watchfield	948	10 A4
Waterperry	181	11 F2
Waterstock	89	11 F2
Watlington	2,159	11 G4
Wendlebury	371	9 E5
West Challow	210	10 C4
West End		10 D2
West Ginge		10 D5
West Hagbourne	312	11 E5
West Hanney	490	10 C4
West Hendred	342	10 D4
Westcott Barton	159	8 D4
Weston on the Green	479	9 E5
Westwell	61	8 A6
Wheatfield	31	*
Wheatley	3,506	11 F2
Whitchurch	839	11 F6
Whitchurch Hill		11 F6
Wiggington	196	8 C3
Williamscot		8 D2
Witney	14,343	10 C2
Wolvercote		10 D2
Woodcote	2,458	11 F5
Woodeaton	71	9 E6
Woodstock	3,268	8 D6
Woolstone	108	10 B5
Wootton	639	8 D5
Wootton	2,628	10 D3
Worton	96	*
Wroxton	556	8 C2
Wytham	152	10 D2
Yarnton	2,297	8 D6
Yelford (with Hardwick)	103	10 C2

Population figures (in bold type) are based upon the 1981 census and relate to the local authority area or parish as constituted at that date. Places with no population figure form part of a larger local authority area or parish. District boundaries are shown on pages 4 and 5.
* Parish not shown on map pages 8-11 due to limitation of scale.

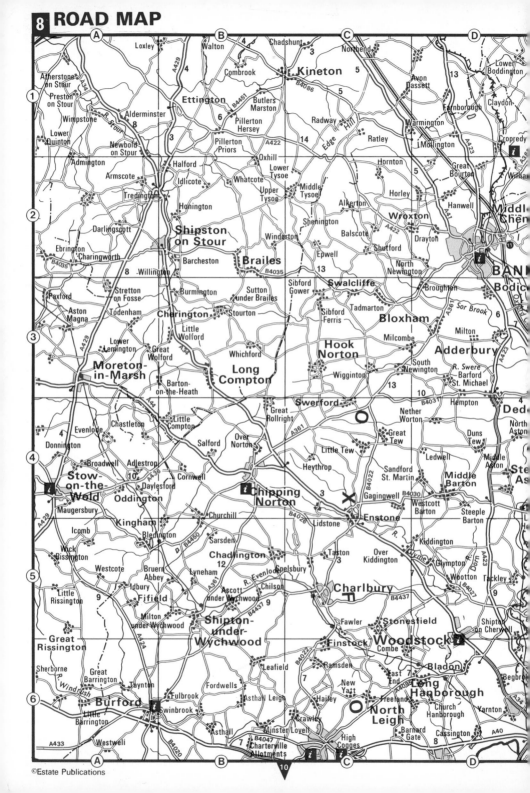

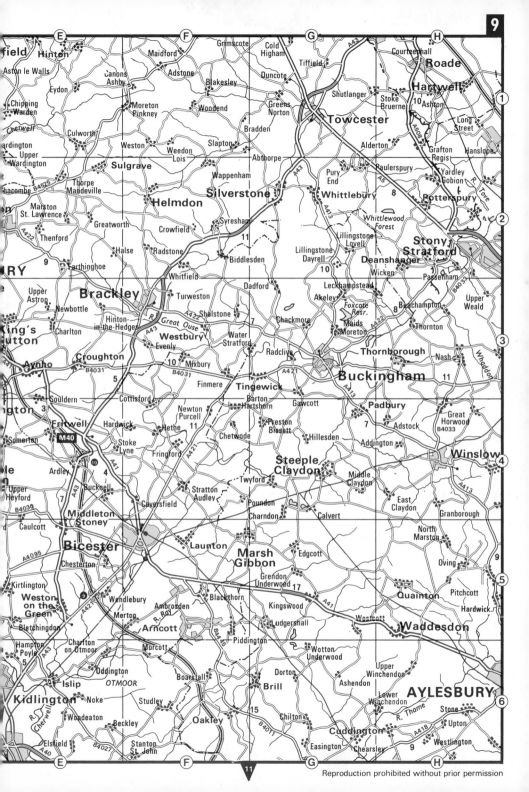

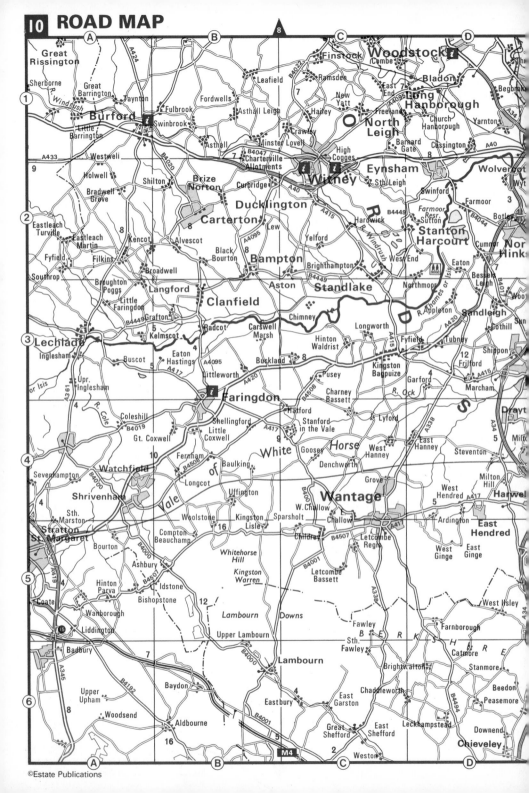

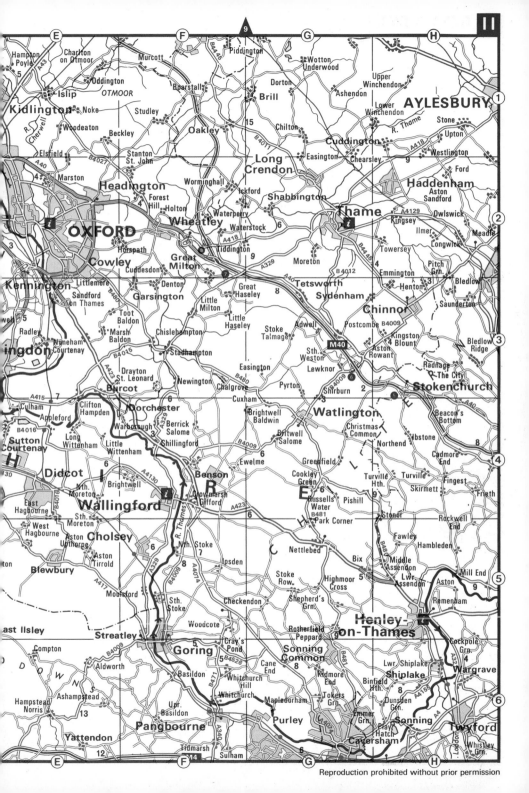

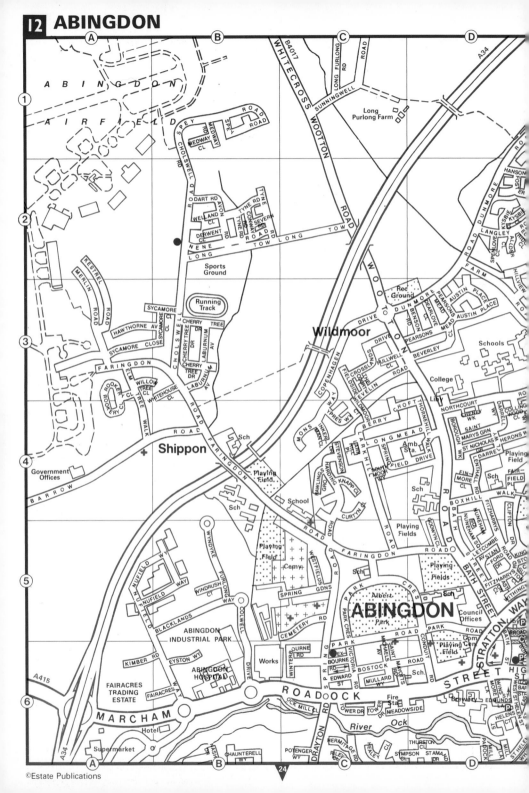

St. Peters College

Peach Croft Farm

Peachcroft

Northcourt

Sports Ground

Peachcroft Shopping Centre

Barrow Hills

RADLEY ROAD INDUSTRIAL ESTATE

Wick Hall

Schools

Bow-Grave Copse

The Copse

ABINGDON SCIENCE PARK

Wick Hall Gravel Pits

Recreation Ground

Works

Thames View Industrial Park

Abbey Gardens

Abbey Meadow

River Thames

Guildhall

Pol. Sta.

Old Gaol / Rec Cen

Rye Farm

Sports Ground

25

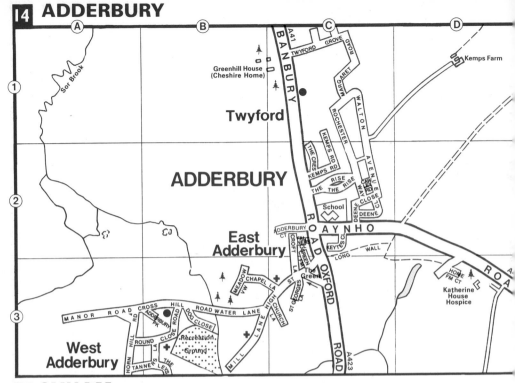

Twyford

ADDERBURY

Greenhill House
(Cheshire Home)

Kemps Farm

East Adderbury

The Green

Katherine House Hospice

School

West Adderbury

Recreation Ground

BLOXHAM

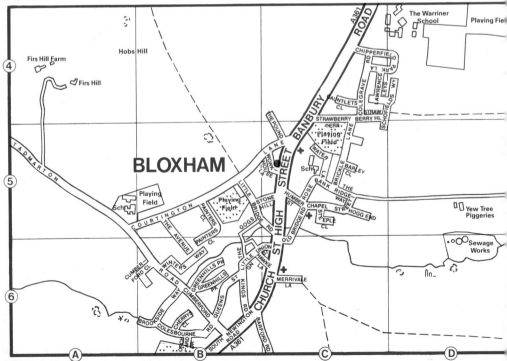

Firs Hill Farm

Firs Hill

Hobs Hill

The Warriner School

Playing Field

BLOXHAM

Playing Field

Playing Field

Yew Tree Piggeries

Sewage Works

©Estate Publications

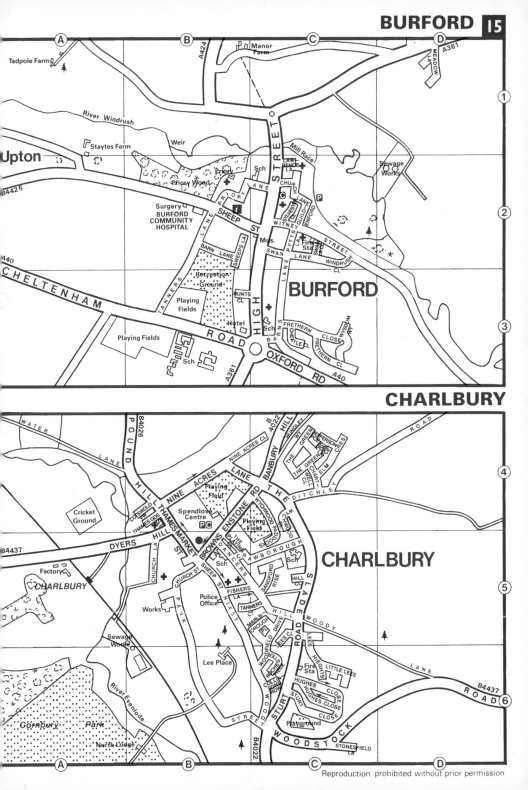

CHARLBURY

16 BANBURY

©Estate Publications

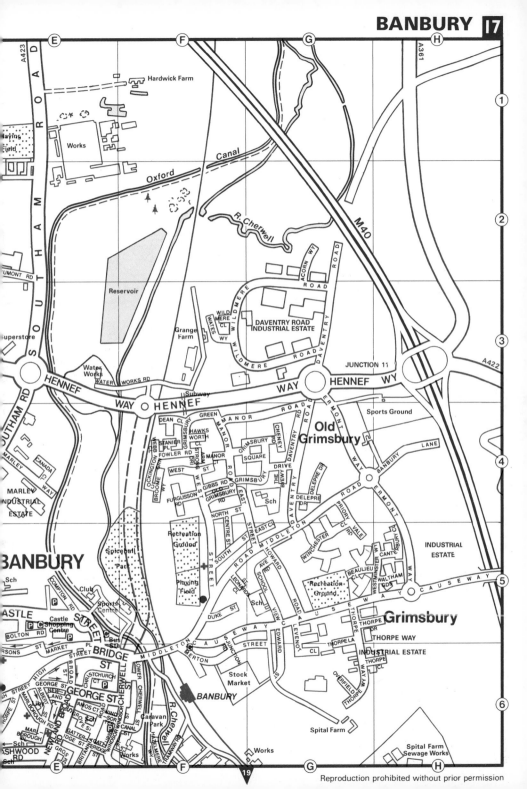

BANBURY 17

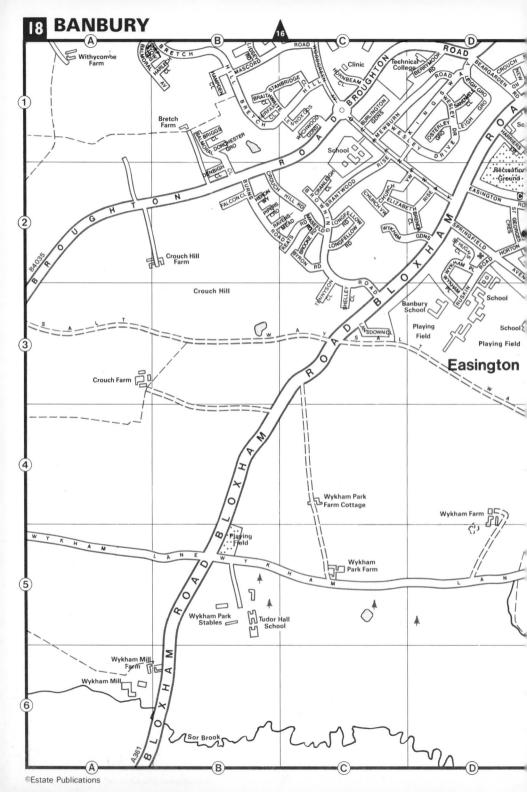

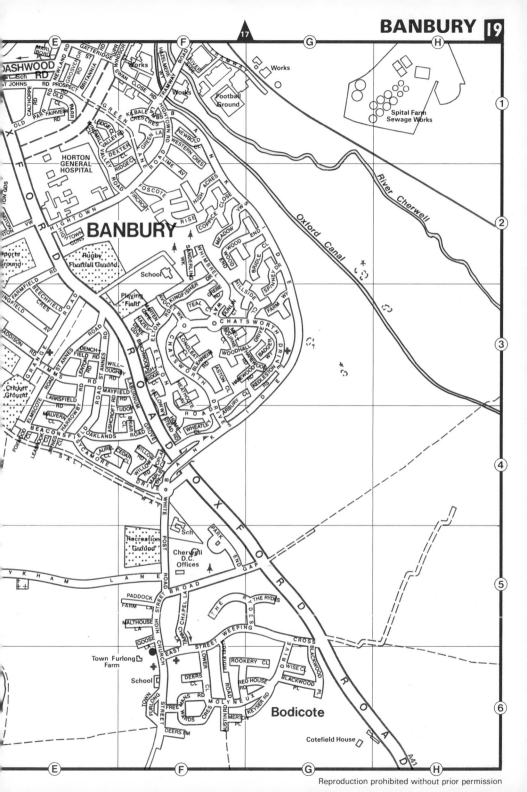

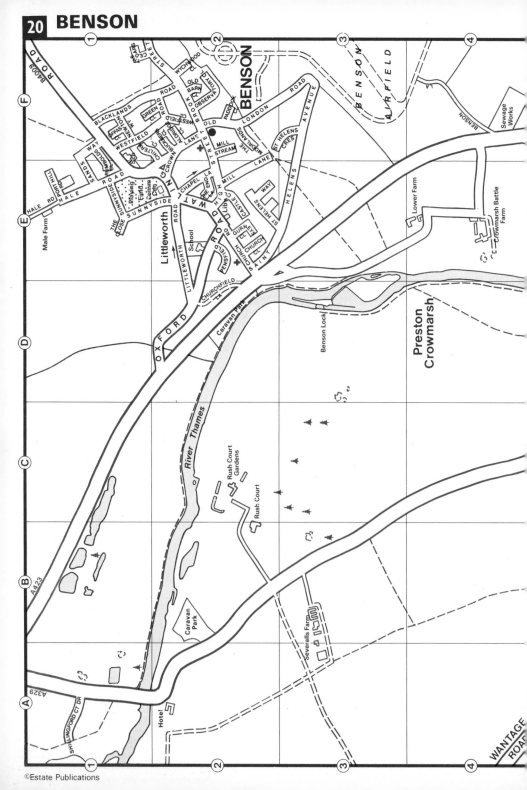

BENSON

Benson Airfield

Sewage Works

Crowmarsh Battle Farm

Lower Farm

Crowmarsh

St Helens Cres

London Road

Avenue

The Moorlands

Paddock

Old Mill

Mill Stream

St Helens Lane

Helens Avenue

Observatory

Old Barn

Wychwood

Oxgate

Crown Street

Blacklands

Westfield

Green Close

Chiltern Rd

Aldret Rd

Chapel Lane

The End Lane

High Street

Old Street

Littleworth Road

Oxford Road

Watlington Road

Castle Square

Gurnard CL

Penshel Way

Church Way

St Helens Road

Church CL

School

Littleworth CA

Churchfield CA

Churchfield

Penshel Field

Saint

Sands

Chiltern Way

Rolls Rd

Saffords

Sunnyside Road

The Close

Playing Field

Corina Cen

Benson Lock

Caravan Park

B4009 ROAD

Hale Rd

Port Hill

HALE

Male Farm

A423

Shillingford Ct Dr

A329

Caravan Park

Hotel

River Thames

Rush Court Gardens

Rush Court

Preston Crowmarsh

Severalls Farm

WANTAGE ROAD

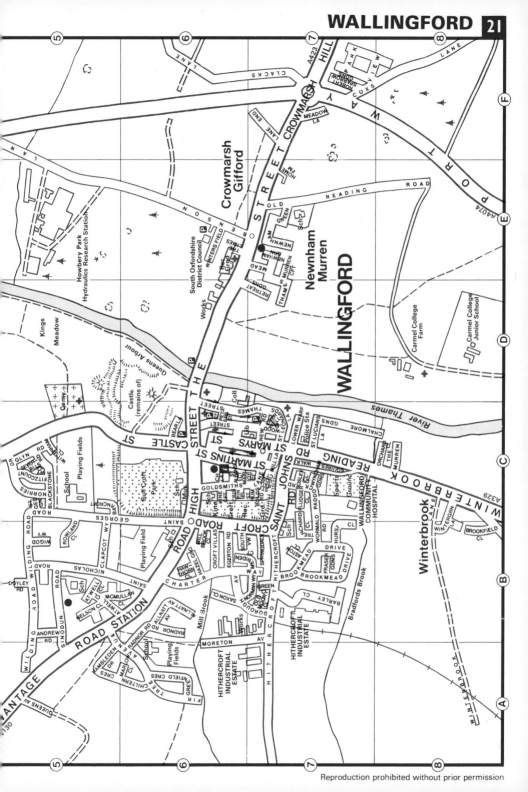

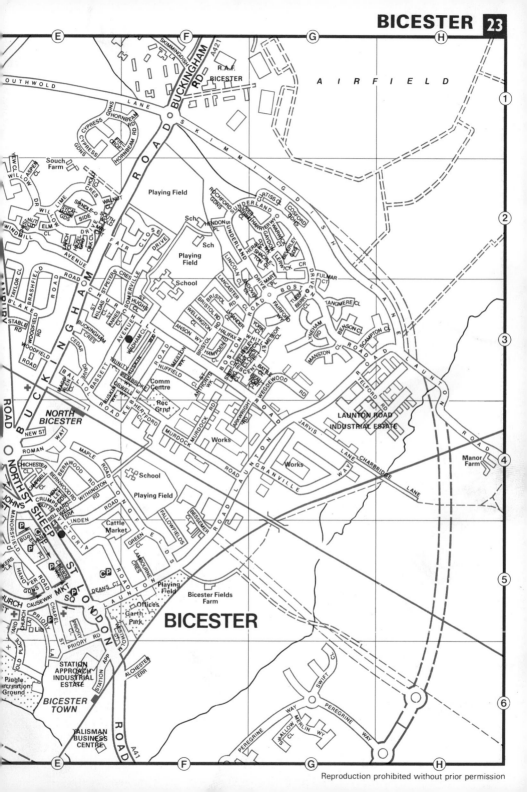

AIRFIELD

R.A.F. BICESTER

BICESTER

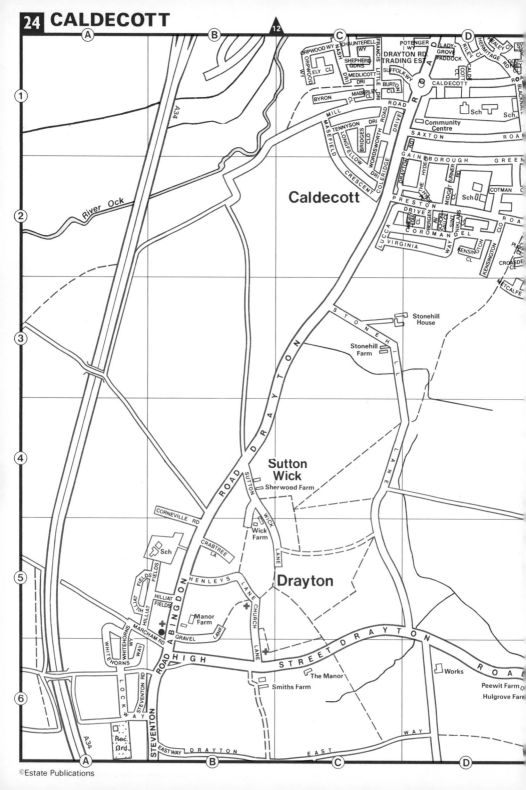

Caldecott

Sutton Wick

Drayton

Stonehill House

Stonehill Farm

Sherwood Farm

Wick Farm

Manor Farm

The Manor

Smiths Farm

Works

Peewit Farm

Hulgrove Farm

Community Centre

River Ock

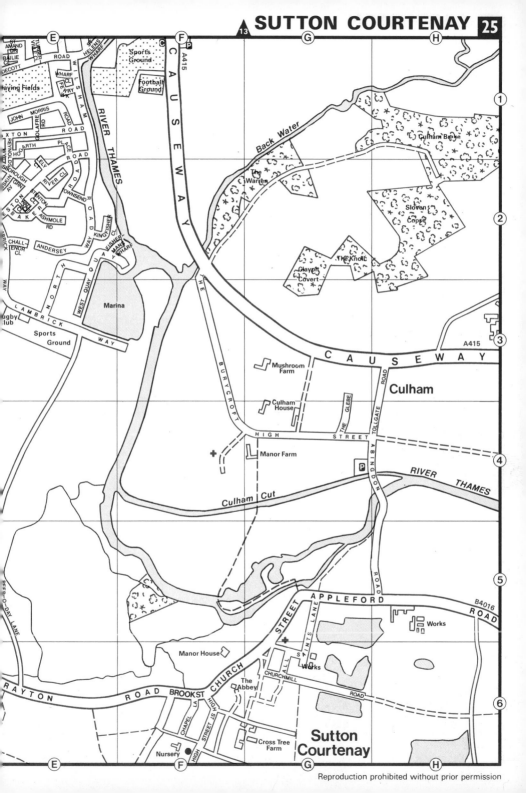

Culham

Sutton Courtenay

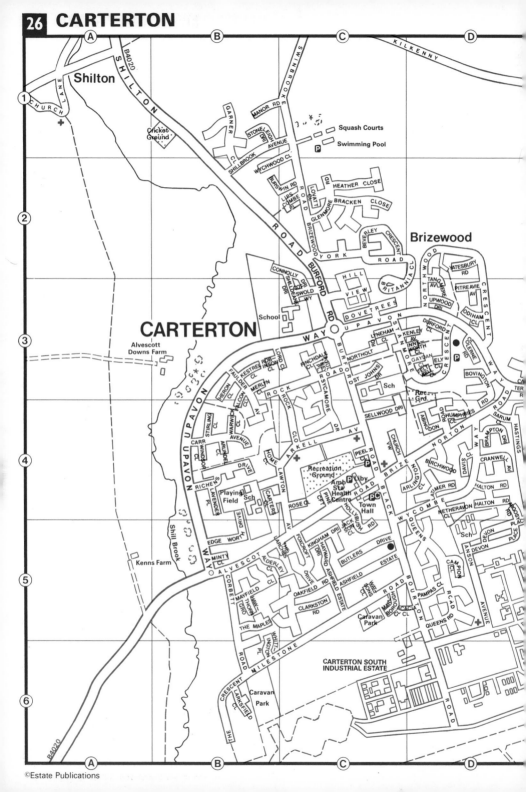

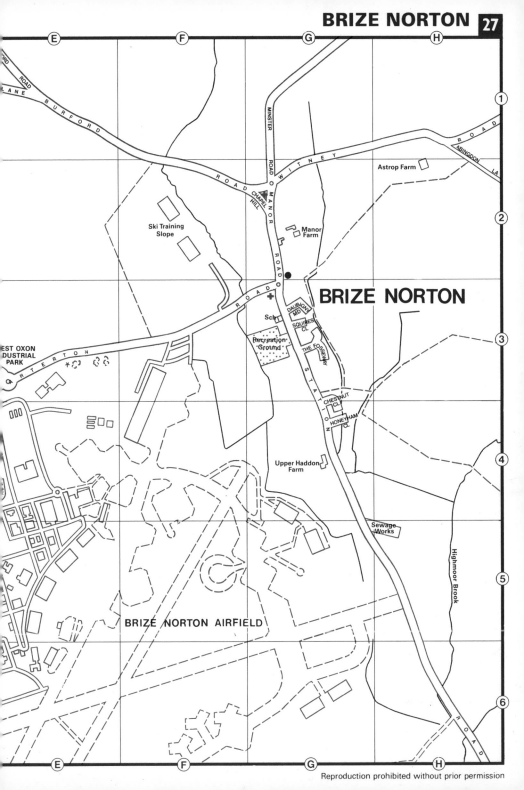

BURFORD ROAD
LANE

MINSTER ROAD

WITNEY ROAD

ABINGDON LA

ROAD

CHAPEL HILL

Astrop Farm

Ski Training Slope

MANOR ROAD

Manor Farm

BRIZE NORTON

WEST OXON INDUSTRIAL PARK

CARTERTON ROAD

Sch

Recreation Ground

DAUBIGNY MD

SQUIRES CL

THE FOSSEWAY

STATION

CHESTNUT CL

HONEYHAM CL

Upper Haddon Farm

Sewage Works

Highmoor Brook

BRIZE NORTON AIRFIELD

ROAD

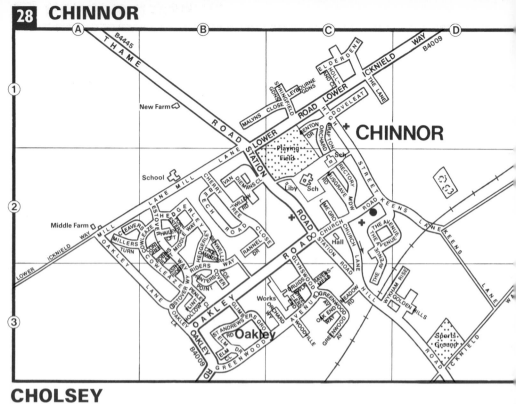

CHOLSEY

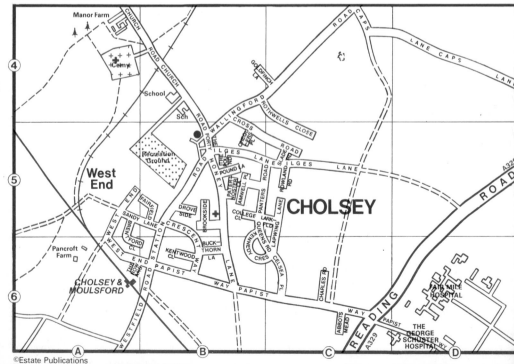

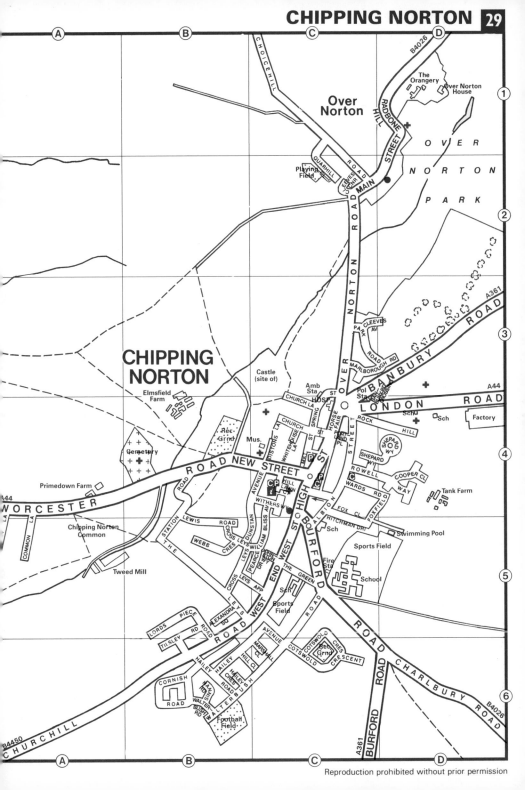

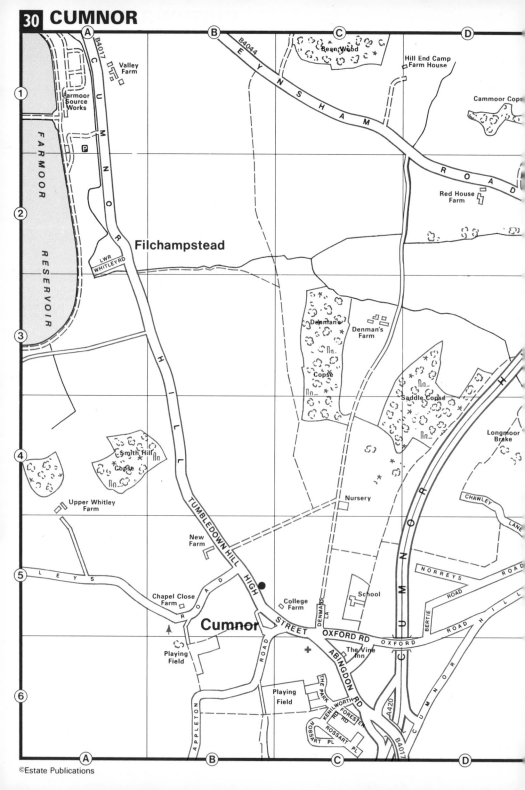

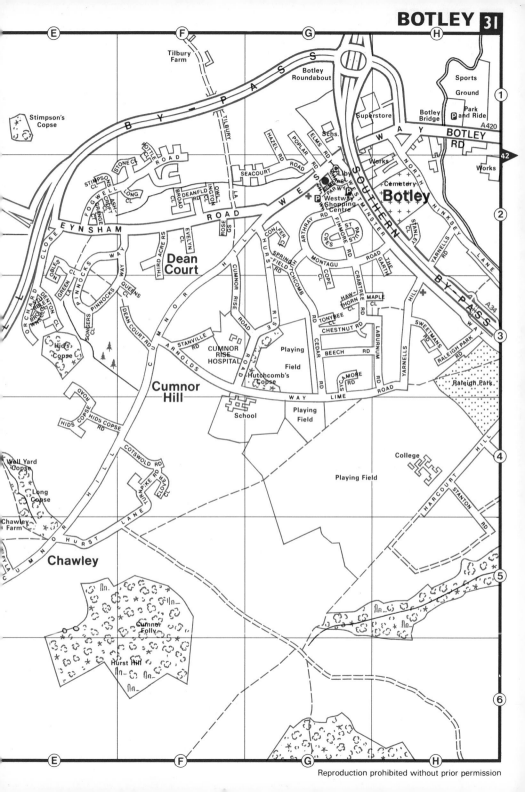

DIDCOT

©Estate Publications

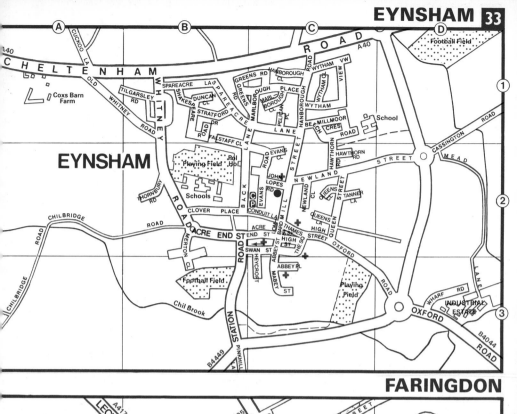

FARINGDON

Grove

Grove Park

Medieval Village of Tulwick

Tulwick Farm

Crab Hill

GROVE PARK DRIVE

A338

Janssen

Crabhill Lane

Gipsy Lane

Henney Bridge

Grove Wick Farm

Monk's Farm

STATION RD

MAYFIELD CL

7TH DRI

GODFREYS WY

COLLIN-SMITH DRI

HOWARD ST

ST JOHNS

OXFORD LANE

MINNS RD

LINDEN CRES

MEADOW CL

ROAD

GLEBE GS

VALE AVE

CAUDWELL

AVENUE

CHERRY TREE CL

HARLINGTON

ST IVES RD

MAYFIELD AV

FLORAL CL

HAWTHORNE CRES

LAUREL DRI

MILES

Grove School

VICARAGE LA

EASTERFIELD

Clinic

BOSLEYS ORCHARD

ST IVES LA

KINGS

FISHERS

SPARLAND

MANDH

Grove Bridge Farm

BRIDGE FM

Elm Farm

GROVE RD

WESTFIELD

Westfield Caravan Park

Recreation Ground

Grove

WICK GRN

WESTBROOK

OLD MILL

Hall

Grove City Centre

Millbrook School

HARDWELL

WAYLAND RD

LIMETREE

EDDINGTON

ROSEBAY CRES

ELSWITH

MEMBURY WY

CHARBURY GRN

POUND CL

REGAL WY

ASH WY

OWN

TUBBS CL

WICKS GREEN FARM

NOBLES

BRUNEL CRES

DENCHWORTH ROAD

STEPTOE CL

THE MAPLES

COW LANE

COTTRELLS MEAD

HERDS

PERRYFIELDS

TOLLETT WY

KESTRELS

SHEPHERDS

SWAN

FULMAR WY

MALLARD

EVENLODE CL

COLNE

WINDRUSH

MANDARIN PL

KENNETT

WOODGATE

MARSH

BROADWAY CL

WOODHILL

FAIRFIELD DRI

MORLAND

FARM CL

BARBURY CRES

ARABLE

ALBERT

NEWLANDS

DRI

BLENHEIM GDS

SAVILE WAY

COLUMBIA WY

WHITE HORSE

HUNTERS

PRINCESS GS

BOWLING

CANE

ROAD

ROAD

DENCHWORTH

Denchworth Road Bridges

Vantage Research Laboratory

EUSTON

STEPHENSON AV

FARADAY RD

GOWER

NEWTON

MAXWELL WAY

©Estate Publications

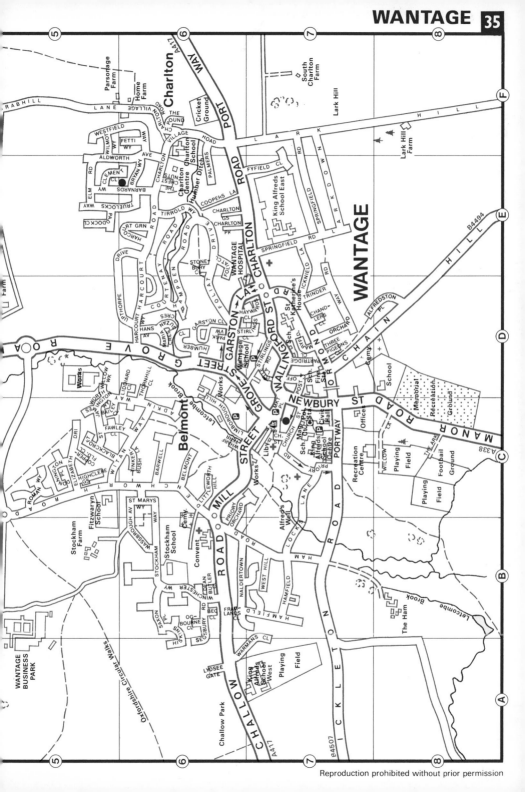

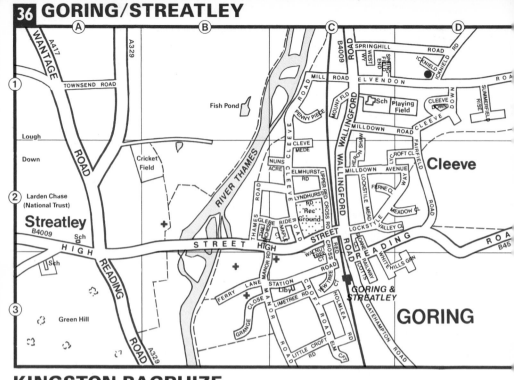

KINGSTON BAGPUIZE

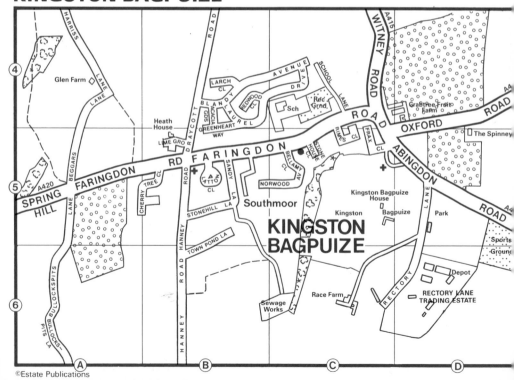

©Estate Publications

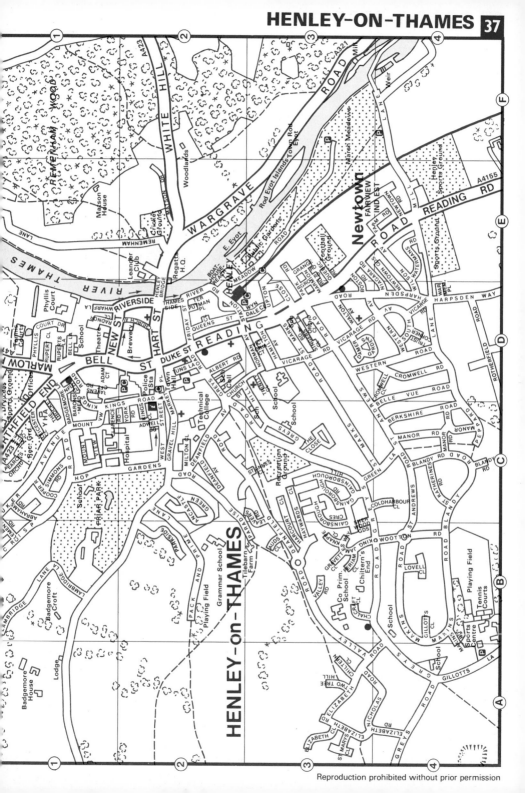

HENLEY-on-THAMES

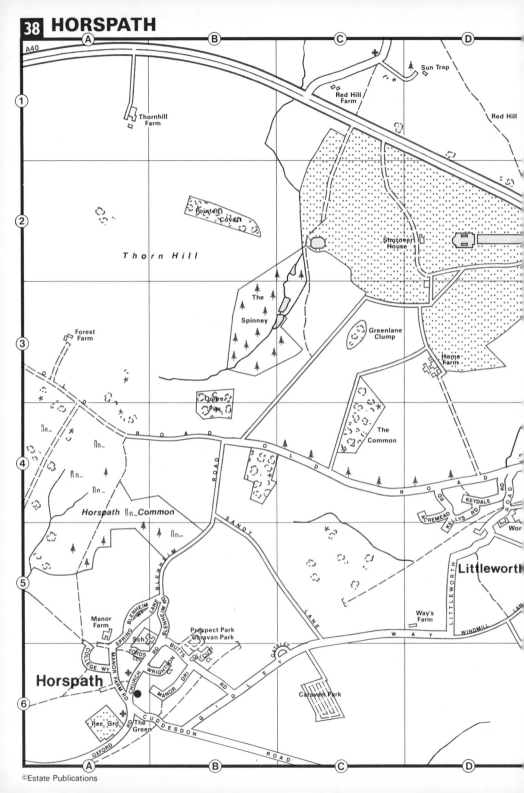

A40

Thornhill Farm

Sun Trap

Red Hill Farm

Red Hill

Pointers Covert

Thorn Hill

Strotover House

The Spinney

Greenlane Clump

Home Farm

Forest Farm

Gravel Pits

R O A D

The Common

KEYDALE

ACREMEAD

KELLYS RD

RD

ROAD

RD

Wor

Horspath Common

SANDY LANE

LITTLEWORTH

Littleworth

Manor Farm

BLENHEIM LANE

BLENHEIM RD

SPRING CL

Sch

FORDS CL

COLLEGE WY

Prospect Park Caravan Park

BUTTS

WRIGHTSON CL

CL COURT CL

Way's Farm

WINDMILL LANE

W A Y

Horspath

MANOR FARM RD

CHURCH

MANOR DRI

GIDLEY RD

GIDLEY WAY

Caravan Park

Rec. Grd.

The Green

OXFORD RD

C U D D E S D O N

R O A D

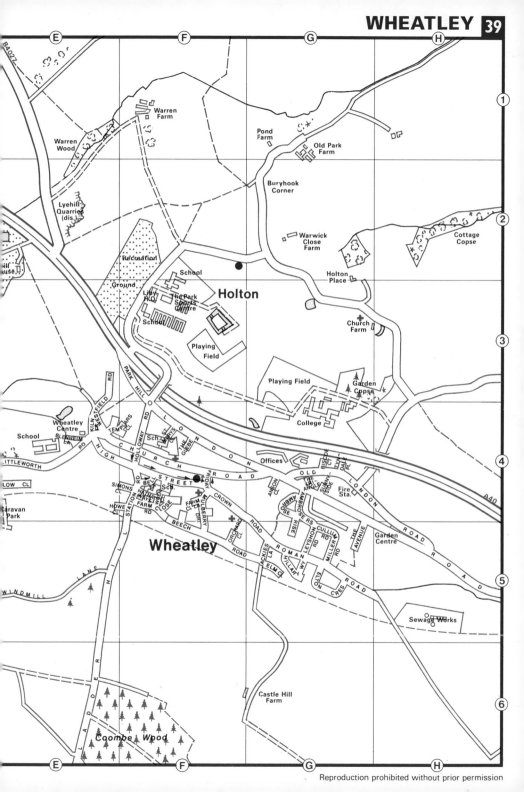

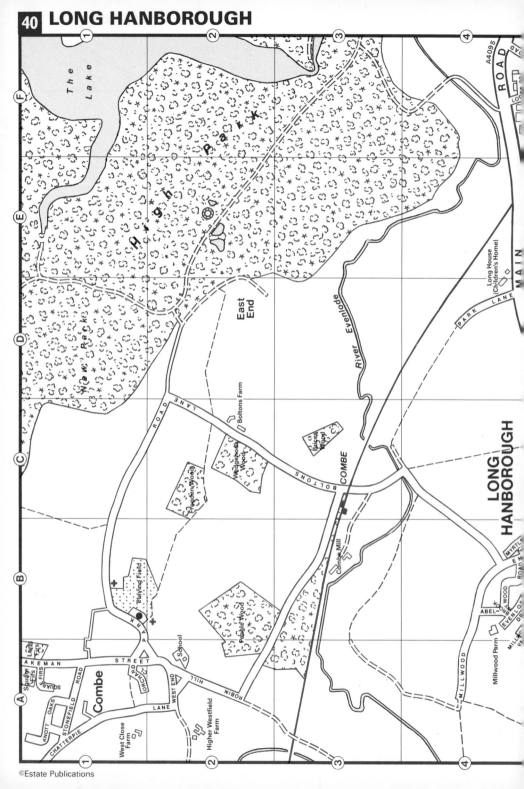

The Lake

High Park

New Park's

East End

River Evenlode

Long House (Children's Home)

MAIN

A4095 ROAD

PARK LANE

Boltons Farm

Baines Wood

COMBE

BOLTONS

Wedgehog Wood

Pagden Wood

Combe Mill

LONG HANBOROUGH

LANE ROAD

Playing Field

School

Peaple Wood

MILLWOOD

Millwood Farm

MYRTLE

EVENLODE WOOD

ABEL WOOD

Square FIRS

AKEMAN STREET

WEST END

Combe

STONEFIELD ROAD

ORCHARD ROAD

ROBIN HILL

KNOTT OAKS

CHATTERPIE LANE

West Close Farm

Higher Westfield Farm

©Estate Publications

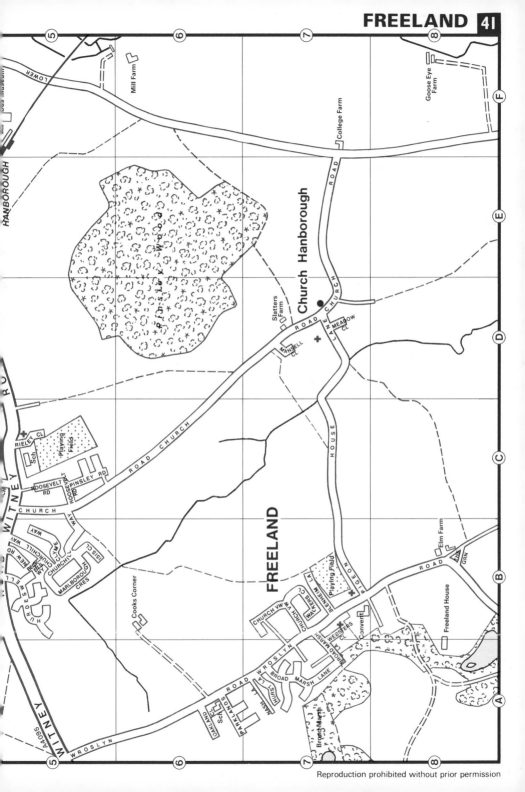

©Estate Publications

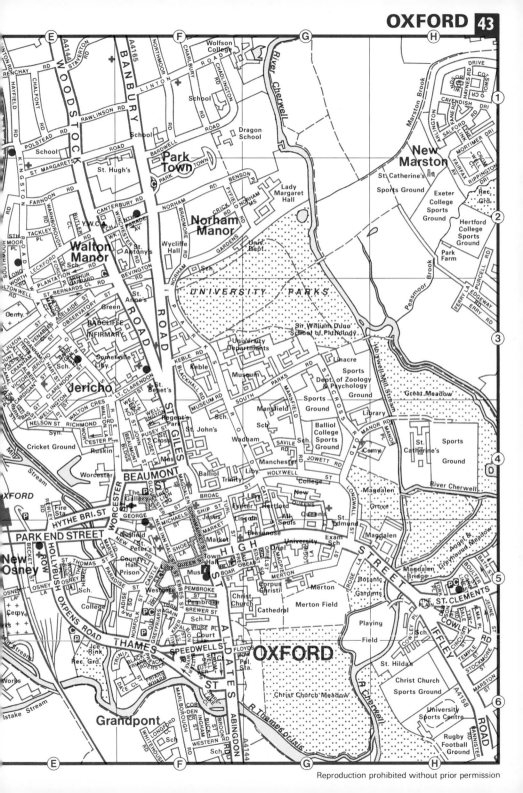

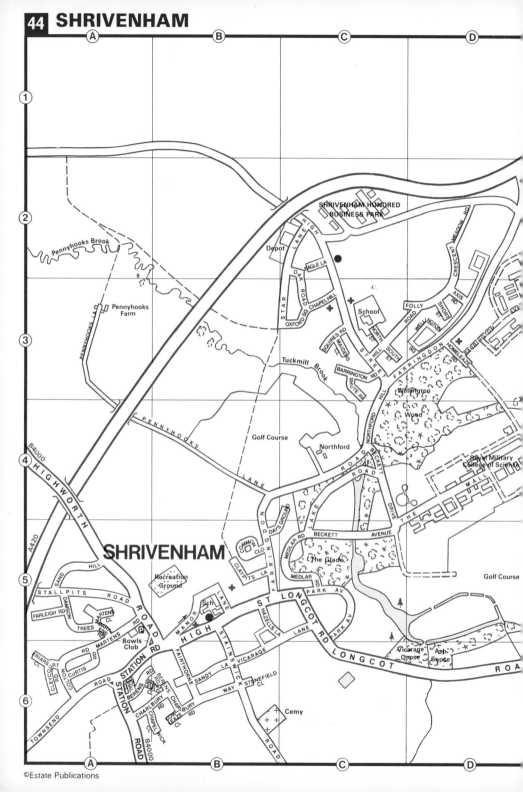

E F G H

1
2
3
4
5
6

A420

KINGS

ST HUGHS CRES

MALLINS LANE

LANE

School

Longcot

CHURCH

SHRIVENHAM RD

B4508

FERNHAM RD

A JORS

BOWER GREEN

BOWER GREEN

AVENUE

Little Wellington Wood

WATCHFIELD

Bower Copse

Bower Brook

SHRIVENHAM ROAD

Cleveland Farm

Stone Farm

OLD

ROAD

WHARF

ROAD

Broadleaze Farm

Home Farm

LONGCOT

Gallyherns Farm

VALE OF WHITE HORSE

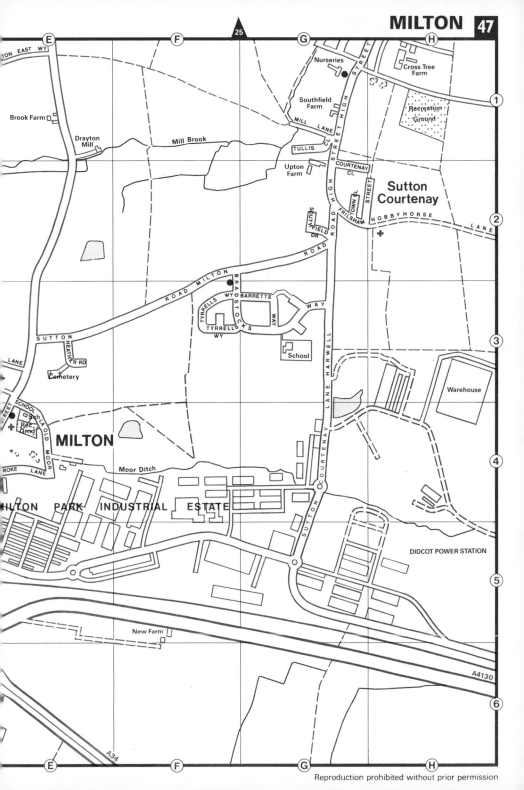

25

E F G H

TON EAST WY

Brook Farm

Drayton Mill

Mill Brook

Nurseries

Cross Tree Farm

Southfield Farm

MILL LANE

TULLIS

Upton Farm

COURTENAY CL

Recreation Ground

HIGH STREET

Sutton Courtenay

HOBBYHORSE LANE

SOUTH FIELD DR

ROAD

FRILSHAM STREET

ROAD MILTON

TYRRELLS WY

BRADSTOCKS

BARRETTS

TYRRELLS WY

WAY

WAY

School

SUTTON

HEATHER RD

Cemetery

LANE

SCHOOL

Sch La OLD MOOR

STREET

Rec Grnd

MILTON

ROKE LANE

Moor Ditch

HARWELL LANE

Warehouse

COURTENAY LANE

SUTTON

MILTON PARK INDUSTRIAL ESTATE

DIDCOT POWER STATION

New Farm

A4130

A34

E F G H

(1)
(2)
(3)
(4)
(5)
(6)

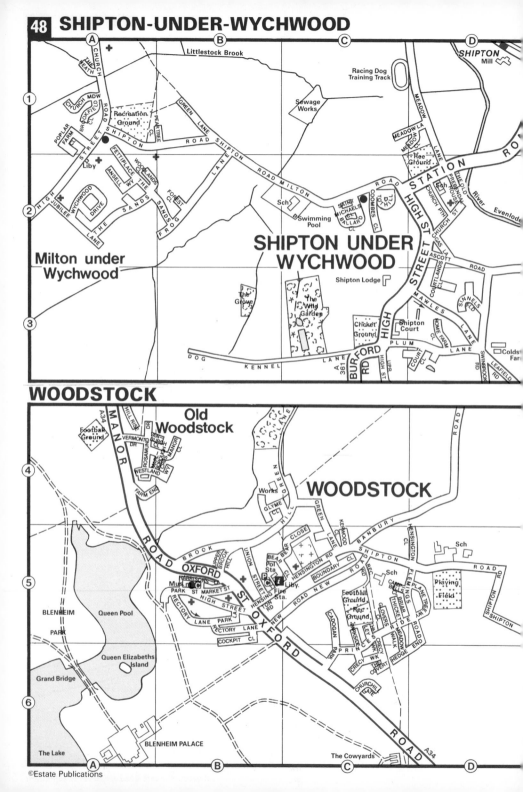

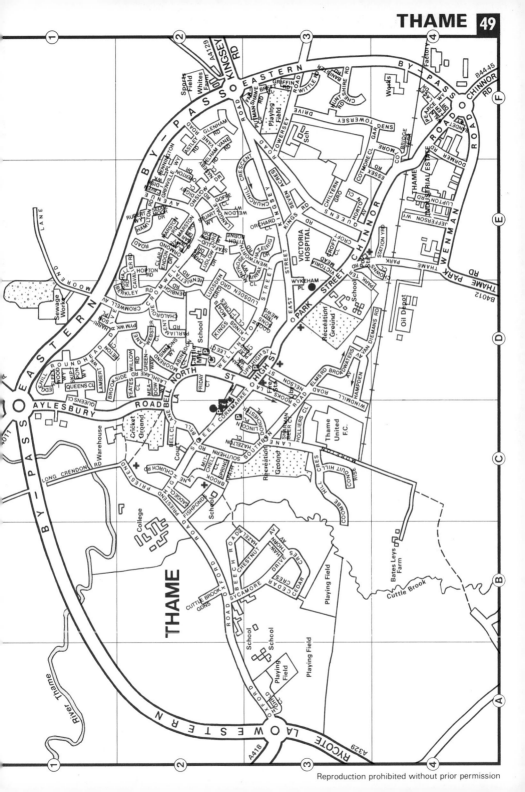

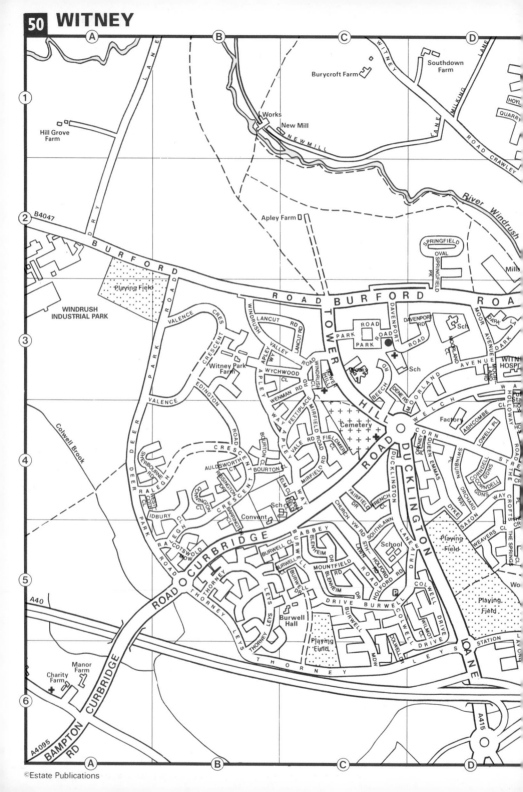

50 WITNEY

©Estate Publications

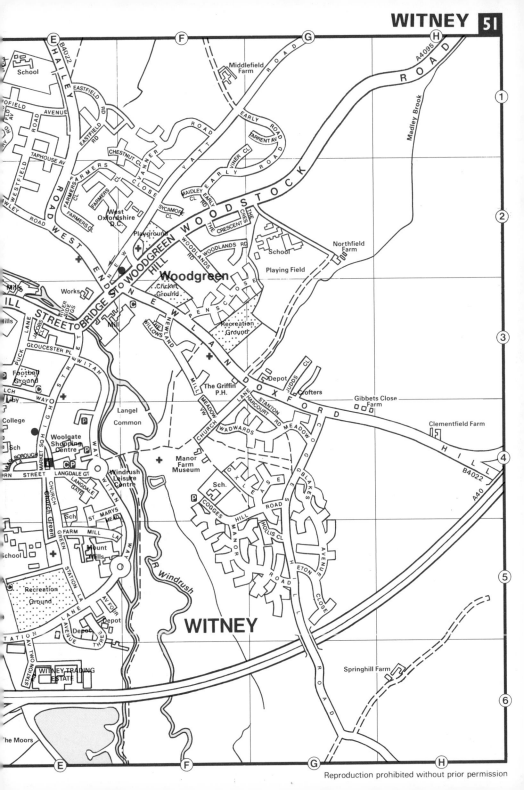

WITNEY

Woodgreen

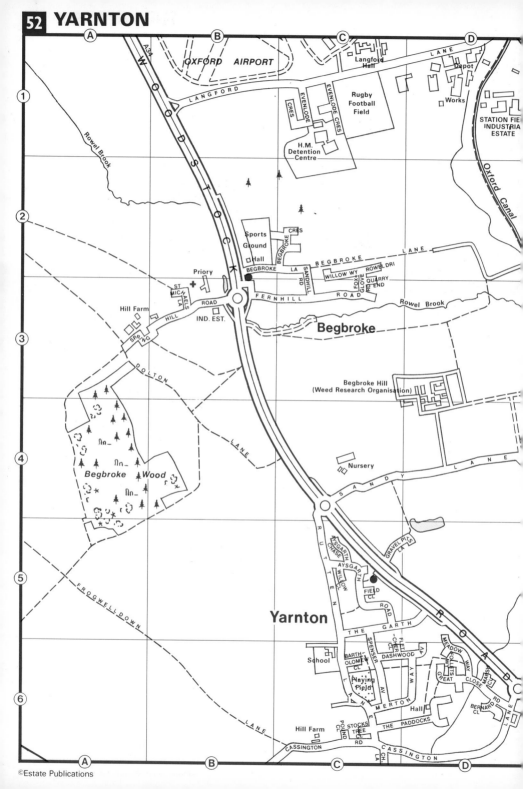

OXFORD AIRPORT

Langford Hall

LANGFORD LANE

Depot

Works

STATION FIE
INDUSTRIA
ESTATE

Rowel Brook

LANGFORD

Oxford Canal

EVENLODE CRES

EVENLODE CRES

Rugby
Football
Field

H.M.
Detention
Centre

Sports
Ground

Hall

CRES

BEGBROKE LA

Priory

BEGBROKE LANE

WILLOW WY

FOX GLOVE

ROWEL DRI

QUARRY
END

St
MICHAELS
LA

HILL

ROAD

IND. EST.

Hill Farm

SPRING

FERNHILL

ROAD

Rowel Brook

Begbroke

DOLTON

Begbroke Hill
(Weed Research Organisation)

LANE

Begbroke Wood

Nursery

SANDY

LANE

FROGWELL DOWN

RUTTEN

AYSGARTH
CHASE

AYSGARTH

WILLOW

FIELD
CL

GRAVEL PITS
LA

ROAD

Yarnton

THE GARTH

SPENSER AV

FLEET
CL

CHERRY

DASHWOOD

MEADOW WAY

School

BARTH-
OLOMEW
CL

WILLOW WAY

FOLLETS CLOSE

GREAT

WAY

RA

Haying
Field

MERTON

AV

LANE

Hall

BERNARD
CL

Hill Farm

PO

STOCKS
TREE
CL

THE PADDOCKS

CL CH

POND

RD

CASSINGTON

CASSINGTON

LANE

INDEX TO STREETS

ABINGDON

Street	Ref
Abbey Clo	13 E6
Abbott Rd	13 E5
Abingdon Ind Park	12 B5
Abingdon Science Park	13 G5
Alexander Clo	13 F1
Allder Clo	12 D2
Anyce Clo	13 G2
Appleford Dri	13 F2
Ashenden Clo	13 E4
Aston Clo	12 D5
Audlett Dri	13 E5
Austin Pl	12 D3
Avon Rd	12 B2
Ballard Chase	13 E1
Barkfleur Clo	13 G2
Barrow Hill Clo	13 G3
Barrow Rd	12 A4
Barton La	13 F5
Bath St	12 D4
Beagle Clo	13 G2
Benson Rd	12 D3
Berry Croft	12 C4
Beverley Clo	12 D3
Blacklands Way	12 B5
Boreford Rd	13 F2
Borough Walk	12 D4
Bostock Rd	12 C6
Boulter Dri	13 E1
Bowgrave Copse	13 G3
Bowyer Rd	13 E4
Boxhill Rd	13 E4
Boxhill Walk	12 D4
Boxwell Clo	13 F2
Bridge St	13 E6
Broad St	12 D5
Brode Clo	13 F2
Brookside	13 E3
Bucklersbury Rd	13 F2
Bury St	12 D6
Buscot Dri	13 F3
Cameron Av	13 G3
Campion Rd	13 G4
Carse Clo	13 F2
Causeway	13 E6
Cemetery Rd	12 C5
Champs Clo	13 G3
Chandlers Clo	13 G3
Charney Av	13 G2
Chaunterell Way	12 B6
Cherry Tree Dri	12 B3
Cherwell Clo	13 F4
Childrey Way	13 F2
Chilton Clo	13 F3
Cholswell Rd	12 B1
Clarendon Clo	13 G5
Clevelands	13 E4
Clifton Dri	12 D5
Collingwood Clo	12 D4
Colwell Dri	12 B5
Compton Dri	13 F2
Conduit Rd	12 D6
Conway Rd	12 B2
Copenhagen Dri	12 C3
Cornavil Clo	13 G3
Covent Clo	13 G2
Creney Walk	12 D4
Crosslands Dri	12 C3
Cullerne Clo	13 E2
Curtis Av	13 F5
Curtyn Clo	12 C4
Daisy Bank	13 G4
Darrell Way	12 D4
Dart Rd	12 B2
Dearlove Clo	12 D3
Denton Clo	13 F5
Derwent Clo	12 B2
Dorchester Cres	13 F3
Duffield Clo	13 F3
Dundas Clo	13 F5
Dunmore Rd	12 C3

Street	Ref
Eason Dri	13 G4
East St Helen St	12 D6
Eden Gro	13 F2
Edward St	12 C6
Eldridge Clo	12 D2
Elizabeth Av	13 G2
Elm Tree Walk	12 A3
Elwes Clo	13 F5
Eney Clo	13 G3
Ethelhem Clo	13 G2
Evelin Rd	12 C3
Evenlode Pk	13 G3
Exbourne Rd	12 C6
Eyston Way	12 B6
Fairacres	12 B6
Fairacres Trading Est	12 A6
Fairfield Pl	12 D4
Faringdon Rd	12 A3
Farm Rd	12 D2
Fennel Way	13 G4
Ferguson Pl	13 G5
Fieldside	12 C3
Finmore Clo	12 D4
Fitzharrys Rd	12 D4
Foster Rd	12 D2
Franklyn Clo	13 E2
Fullwell Clo	12 C3
Gall Clo	13 G5
Galley Field	13 F4
Gardiner Clo	13 G4
Garford Clo	13 F3
Geoffrey Barbour Rd	13 E4
Ginge Clo	13 G2
Glyme Clo	13 F3
Godwyn Clo	12 D5
Gordon Dri	13 G3
Hadland Rd	13 G4
Hamble Dri	13 G3
Hanson Rd	12 D2
Harcourt Way	12 D4
Harding Rd	12 C4
Hart Clo	13 G5
Hawthorne Av	12 A3
Healey Clo	12 C6
Hean Clo	13 F2
Heathcote Pl	13 G4
Hedgemead Av	13 G3
Hendred Way	13 F3
Henor Mill Clo	13 F2
Herman Clo	13 F5
Hermitage Rd	12 C6
Herons Walk	12 D4
High St	12 D6
Hillview Rd	12 D3
Hobbs Clo	13 F5
Holland Rd	13 E3
Holywell Clo	13 G2
Hound Clo	13 G3
Hunter Clo	13 F2
Inkerman Clo	12 C4
Isis Clo	13 G3
John Mason Rd	13 E4
Kempster Clo	13 F5
Kennet Rd	13 F3
Kent Clo	13 G5
Kestrel Rd	12 A3
Kimber Rd	12 A6
Kingston Clo	12 D5
Knapp Clo	12 C4
Kysbie Clo	12 D2
Laburnum Av	12 B3
Lammas Clo	13 E4
Langley Rd	12 D2
Larkhill Clo	12 C4
Larkhill Pl	12 C4
Lee Av	13 F5
Lenthall Rd	12 D4
Letcombe Av	12 D5
Levery Clo	13 G4

Street	Ref
Lindsay Dri	13 F3
Loddon Clo	13 F3
Lombard St	12 D6
Long Furlong Rd	12 C1
Long Tow	12 B2
Longmead	12 C4
Lumberd Rd	13 F2
Lyford Way	13 F2
Lynges Clo	13 G2
Lyon Clo	13 E3
Mandeville Clo	13 E2
Marcham Rd	12 A6
Market Sq	13 E6
Mattock Way	13 F2
Mayotts Rd	12 C6
Meadowside	12 C6
Medway Clo	12 B1
Medway Rd	12 B1
Merlin Rd	12 A3
Mill La	12 D6
Mill Padock	12 D6
Minchins Clo	13 G4
Mons Way	12 C4
Morton Clo	13 G5
Mullard Way	12 C6
Myatt Rd	13 G5
Nash Dri	12 B6
Nene Rd	12 B2
New St	13 E5
Norbrook Clo	13 G2
Norman Av	13 E4
Norris Clo	13 G3
North Av	13 E2
Northcourt La	13 E3
Northcourt Rd	12 D4
Northcourt Way	13 E4
Northfield Rd	13 E2
Nufield Way	12 A5
Nuneham Sq	12 D5
Ock Mill Clo	12 C6
Ock St	12 C6
Old Farm Clo	13 G5
Orchard Clo	13 E4
Otwell Clo	13 F2
Oxford Rd	13 E5
Pagisters Rd	13 G3
Park Cres	12 C5
Park Rd	12 C6
Peachcroft Rd	13 G2
Pearsons Mead	12 D3
Penn Clo	13 G2
Picklers Hill	13 E3
Potenger Way	12 C6
Prince Gro	13 E1
Purslane	13 G4
Pykes Clo	13 F2
Pytenry Clo	13 F2
Queen St	12 D6
Radley Rd	13 E5
Radley Rd Ind Est	13 F4
Rainbow Way	13 F2
Ramsons Way	13 G4
Rawlings Gro	12 C4
Reade Av	13 G5
Riley Clo	12 C6
Rivy Clo	13 G4
Rookery Clo	12 A3
Rushmead Copse	13 G2
Saffron Ct	13 G4
St Amand Dri	12 D6
St Andrews Clo	13 G2
St Edmunds La	12 D6
St Helens Ct	12 D6
St Helens Wharf	12 D6
St Johns Rd	13 E4
St Marys Grn	12 D4
St Michaels Av	12 C6
St Nicholas Gr	12 D4
St Peters Rd	13 G3

Street	Ref
Sandford Clo	13 G2
Sellwood Rd	13 E3
Severn Rd	12 B2
Sewell Clo	13 G4
Shelley Clo	13 E3
Sherwood Av	13 F5
Shrives Clo	13 G2
South Av	13 E2
Southmoor Way	12 C4
Spenlove Clo	12 D2
Spey Rd	12 B1
Spring Gdns	12 C5
Spring Rd	12 C6
Springfield Dri	12 C4
Stanford Dri	12 D5
Station Rd	13 E5
Stert St	13 E6
Stevenson Dri	12 C4
Stockey End	13 G2
Stratton Way	12 D6
Sunningwell Rd	12 C1
Sutton Clo	12 D5
Swimburne Rd	13 E4
Sycamore Clo	12 A3
Sympson Clo	12 D6
Tatham Rd	13 E4
Terrington Clo	13 E3
Thames St	13 E6
Thames View Ind Park	13 E5
The Chestnuts	13 G3
The Copse	13 G3
The Court	12 C3
The Grove	13 F2
The Holt	13 E5
The Motte	13 E5
The Warren	13 F5
Thesiger Rd	13 E5
Thistlecroft Clo	13 F2
Thornehill Walk	13 E3
Thurston Clo	12 D6
Tower Dri	12 C6
Trinity Clo	13 F2
Turnagain La	13 E6
Twelve Acre Dri	13 F1
Tyne Rd	12 B2
Upton Clo	13 F3
Victoria Rd	12 C6
Villeboys Clo	13 G4
Vineyard	13 E5
Warwick Clo	13 E4
Waxes Clo	13 G3
Welford Gdns	13 F3
Welland Clo	12 B2
Wellesbourne Clo	13 F5
West Av	13 E2
West St Helen St	12 C5
Westfields	12 C5
Wheatcroft Clo	13 E2
Whitecross	12 C1
Whitehouse Clo	12 B3
Whitelock Rd	13 E4
Wick Clo	13 G2
Wildmoor Ct	12 C4
Willow Tree Clo	12 A3
Windrush Ct	12 B5
Windrush Way	13 F3
Winsmore La	12 D6
Winterbourne Rd	12 C6
Withington Ct	12 D5
Woodley Clo	13 E2
Wootton Rd	12 C1
Wyndyke Furlong	12 B5
Yeld Hall Rd	13 G2
Ypres Way	12 C4

ADDERBURY

Street	Ref
Adderbury Ct	14 C2
Adderbury Park	14 B3
Aynho Rd	14 C2

Street	Ref		Street	Ref		Street	Ref		Street	Ref
Banbury Rd	14 C1		Boxhedge Sq	16 D5		Fairfax Clo	18 B1		Keats Rd	18 C2
Cawley Rd	14 C2		Braithwaite Clo	18 B1		Fairview Rd	19 E1		Keddleston Rise	19 G3
Chapel La	14 B3		Bramber Clo	16 A4		Falcon Clo	18 B2		Kenilworth Way	16 B6
Church La	14 C3		Brantwood Rise	18 C2		Fallow Way	19 F3		Kerry Clo	16 B2
Croft La	14 C2		Brenda Clo	18 D2		Farm Way	19 G3		Keyser Rd	19 G6
Cross Hill Rd	14 B3		Bretch Hill	16 A4		Farmfield Rd	19 E3		Kilbale Cres	19 F1
Deene Clo	14 C2		Briar Clo	19 F4		Ferndale Rd	16 B4		Kingfisher Dri	19 F3
Dog Clo	14 B3		Bridge St	17 E6		Ferriston	16 C3		Kings Rd	16 C6
Falners Clo	14 C2		Bridle Clo	19 G2		Fiennes Rd	16 B6		Kingsway	18 D1
Green Farm	14 C3		Briggs Clo	18 B1		Fircroft	19 F2			
High St	14 C3		Britannia Rd	17 E6		Forgeway	16 C3		Laburnum Gro	19 F3
Home Farm Ct	14 D3		Broad Gap	19 F5		Forsythia Walk	16 C2		Lambs Cres	19 F1
Horn Hill Rd	14 A3		Broad St	17 E6		Foscote Rise	19 F2		Lanchester Dri	16 B3
Kemps Rd	14 C2		Brooke Rd	18 C2		Foundry St	16 D5		Larksfield Rd	19 E3
Keytes Clo	14 C2		Broome Way	17 F4		Fowler Rd	17 F4		Laurel Clo	19 E4
Long Wall	14 C2		Broughton Rd	18 A2		Foxwood Clo	19 E4		Lavender Clo	16 C2
Manor Rd	14 A3		Browning Rd	18 C2		Freemans Rd	19 F6		Leabrook Clo	19 E4
Margaret Rd	14 C1		Burlington Gdns	18 C1		Frensham Clo	16 B2		Leigh Gro	18 D1
Meadow View	14 B3		Burns Rd	18 B2		Furgusson Rd	17 F4		Lennox Gdns	18 C1
Mill La	14 B3		Byron Rd	18 C2		Fushia Walk	16 D2		Lenton Rd	19 E3
Oxford Rd	14 C3								Levenot Clo	17 G5
Rochester Way	14 C1		Caernarvon Way	16 A5		Garden Clo	16 D4		Lidsey Rd	16 B6
Round Close Rd	14 B3		Calthorpe Rd	19 E1		Gatteridge St	19 E1		Lime Av	19 F2
St Georges La	14 C3		Calthorpe St	17 E6		George St	17 E6		Lincoln Clo	16 C6
Tanners La	14 A3		Canada Clo	17 E4		Gibbs Rd	17 F4		Lodge Clo	19 E1
The Cres	14 C2		Canal St	17 F6		Gillett Clo	16 C6		Longelands Way	16 B3
The Leys	14 B3		Canterbury Clo	17 H5		Gillett Rd	16 C6		Longfellow Rd	18 C2
The Rise	14 C2		Castle St	17 E5		Glamis Pl	16 A5		Longleat Clo	19 F3
Twyford Gro	14 C1		Causeway	17 F5		Glanville Gdns	16 C5		Lower Cherwell St	17 F6
Walton Av	14 C1		Cedar Clo	19 F4		Glyndebourne Gdns	16 B2		Lower Clo	19 F6
Water La	14 B3		Centre St	17 F4		Golden Villa Clo	16 C6			
			Chapel La	19 F5		Goodrington Clo	16 C5		Malthouse La	19 F5
BANBURY			Chatsworth Dri	19 F3		Goose La	19 F5		Malvern Clo	19 E4
			Cheney Rd	17 G3		Grange Rd	19 E3		Manor Ct	17 F4
Abbey Rd	16 C5		Chepstow Gdns	16 A6		Grebe Rd	19 F3		Manor Rd	17 F4
Acacia Walk	16 C3		Cherry Rd	16 B5		Green La	19 E1		Maple Ct	19 F4
Acorn Way	17 G2		Cherwell St	17 F6		Greys Clo	16 B5		Margaret Clo	16 B6
Addison Rd	19 E3		Chester Way	16 B5		Grimsbury Dri	17 F4		Market Pl	17 E6
Albert St	17 E6		Chetwode	16 B3		Grimsbury Grn	17 F4		Marlborough Pl	17 E6
Alfriston Pl	16 B2		Cheviot Way	16 B2		Grimsbury Sq	17 G4		Marlborough Rd	17 E6
Alvis Gate	16 B3		Chichester Walk	16 B2		Grosvenor Rd	19 E1		Marley Ind Est	17 E4
Amberly Ct	16 B3		Christchurch Ct	17 E6		Grove St	17 E6		Marley Way	17 E4
Amos Ct	17 E6		Church St	19 F6		Guernsey Way	16 B2		Marlowe Clo	16 B5
Angus Clo	16 B3		Church View	18 C2					Marten Gate	19 F3
Appleby Clo	16 A5		Cockington Grn	17 F4		Hampden Clo	18 B1		Mascord Clo	16 B6
Arbury Clo	19 F4		Compton St	17 E5		Hardwick Park	16 A2		Mascord Rd	16 B6
Armstrong Dri	17 F4		Conifer Rise	16 C2		Harewood Rd	19 F3		Masefield Rd	18 C2
Arran Gro	16 D5		Conway Rd	16 A6		Harlech Clo	16 A6		Mayfield Rd	19 E3
Arundel Pl	16 B6		Cope St	16 D5		Harlequin Way	16 C2		Meadow View	19 F2
Ashcroft Rd	19 E4		Coppice Clo	19 F2		Harriers View	18 D1		Melbourne Clo	19 F3
Ashridge Clo	19 F3		Cranleigh Clo	18 C2		Harrowby Rd	19 E4		Merton Pl	19 F6
Aston Clo	19 F3		Cromwell Rd	16 B5		Hastings Clo	16 A5		Merton St	17 F6
Austin Dri	16 B3		Crouch Hill Rd	18 B2		Hastings Rd	16 A5		Mewburn Rd	18 C1
Austin Rd	19 F6		Crouch St	18 D1		Hawksworth Clo	17 F4		Middleton Rd	17 F6
Avenue Rd	17 G5					Hazeldene Gdns	19 F3		Miller Rd	16 C5
Avocet Walk	19 F3		Daimler Av	16 B3		Hazelmere Way	19 F1		Mold Cres	16 B6
Ayrshire Clo	16 B2		Danesmoor	16 C3		Hearth Way	16 C3		Molyneux Dri	19 F6
Azalea Walk	16 C3		Dashwood Rd	19 E1		Heathcote Av	19 F3		Morgan Clo	16 B3
			Daventry Rd	17 G3		Hennef Way	17 E3		Morris Dri	16 B4
Badger Way	19 G3		Daventry Rd Ind Est	17 G3		Hereford Way	16 B2			
Balmoral Av	16 A6		Deacon Way	16 C6		Heron Way	18 B2		Neithrop Av	16 C4
Balmoral Clo	18 B1		Dean Clo	17 F4		High Acres	19 F2		Neithrop Clo	16 D5
Banbury La	17 H4		Deers Clo	19 F6		High Furlong	16 C3		New Rd	18 D1
Banesberie Clo	16 B3		Deers Farm	19 F6		High St, Banbury	17 E6		Newbold Clo	19 F1
Bankside	19 F1		Delepre Dri	17 G4		High St, Bodicote	19 F5		Newland Pl	17 E6
Barcombe Clo	16 B2		Denbigh Clo	18 B2		Highlands	16 A3		Newland Rd	17 E6
Bath Rd	16 D6		Denchfield Rd	19 E3		Hightown	19 E2		North Bar Pl	16 D5
Beaconsfield Rd	19 E4		Devon Way	16 B3		Hightown Gdns	19 E2		North Bar St	16 D6
Beargarden Rd	18 D1		Dexter Clo	19 E1		Hillside Clo	19 F3		North St	17 F4
Beatrice Dri	16 C6		Dorchester Gro	18 B1		Hillview Cres	16 B4		Nuffield Dri	16 B4
Beaulieu Clo	17 G5		Dover Av	16 A5		Hilton Rd	16 C5		Nursery Dri	16 D4
Beaumaris Clo	16 A4		Duke St	17 F5		Homestead Rd	19 F4		Nursery La	16 D4
Beaumont Clo	16 D2		Dunlin Ct	19 F3		Hornbeam Clo	18 C1			
Beaumont Rd	16 D3					Horse Fair	16 D6		Oaklands Rd	19 E4
Bedford Clo	16 B3		Easington Gdns	19 E2		Horsham Clo	16 A3		Old Clo	19 E1
Beechfield Cres	19 E3		Easington Rd	18 D2		Horton View	18 D2		Old Grimsbury Rd	17 F4
Beesley Rd	16 C5		East Clo	17 G5		Howard Rd	17 G5		Old Parr Rd	19 E1
Bentley Clo	16 A3		East St, Bodicote	19 F6		Humber Walk	16 B3		Orchard Clo	16 C5
Berkeley Clo	16 A4		East St, Old Grimsbury	17 F4		Hydrangea Walk	16 C2		Orchard Way	16 C5
Berrymoor Rd	18 D1		Edinburgh Clo	16 A5					Osterley Gro	18 D1
Bettina Cres	16 C2		Edinburgh Way	16 A5		Ironstones	16 C3		Overfield	17 G6
Birchwood	19 F3		Edmunds Rd	16 B6					Oxford Rd	19 E1
Bird Clo	16 C5		Edward St	17 G5		Japonica Walk	16 C2			
Blackwood Pl	19 G6		Elizabeth Rise	18 C2		Jaynes Clo	19 E4		Paddock Farm Clo	19 F5
Blenheim Rd	19 F3		Elmscote Rd	19 E4		Jersey Dri	16 B2		Park Clo	16 D5
Bloxham Rd	18 A6		Elton Rd	19 F3		Junction Rd	17 F6		Park End	19 F5
Bolton Rd	17 E5		Erica Clo	16 C2		Juniper Clo	16 C2		Park Rd	16 C5
Boxhedge Rd	16 D5		Ermont Way	17 G4					Parsons St	17 E6
Boxhedge Rd West	16 C5		Evenlode	16 C4						

BENSON/WALLINGFORD

BICESTER

Churchill Rd	23 E3	Lincoln Clo	23 F2	Spitfire Clo	23 G3	Orchard Dri	14 B6
Coker Clo	22 B5	Linden Rd	23 E5	Stable Rd	23 E3	Painters Clo	14 B5
Coleridge Clo	22 B2	Loddon Pl	22 C5	Station App	23 E6	Queens St	14 B6
Colne Clo	22 D5	London Rd	23 E5	Station App Ind Est	23 E6	Rose Bank	14 C5
Cosford Gdns	23 G2	Longfellow Clo	22 C3	Sterling Clo	23 F3	Schofields Way	14 C5
Cowper Clo	22 B2	Longfields	23 E4	Stoneburge Cres	22 D4	South Newington Rd	14 B6
Crockwell Clo	22 D4	Lords La	22 C2	Sunderland Dri	23 F2	Steeple Clo	14 C5
Crown Walk	23 E5	Lyneham Rd	23 G3	Swallow Clo	23 G6	Stone Hill	14 C5
Crumps Butts	23 E4	Lysander Clo	23 F3	Swift Clo	22 B3	Strawberry Hill	14 C4
Curtiss Clo	23 G2			Swift Clo	23 G6	Strawberry Ter	14 C4
Cypress Gdns	23 E1	Macauley Clo	22 C3	Sycamore Gdns	23 E2	Tadmarton Rd	14 A5
		MacKenzie Clo	22 C3			The Avenue	14 B5
Danes Rd	22 C4	Magdelen Clo	23 E3	Talisman Bus. Centre	23 E6	The Gogs	14 B6
Deans Ct	23 E5	Manorsfield Rd	23 E4	Tamar Cres	22 B3	The Pound	14 C5
Defiant Clo	23 F3	Manston Clo	23 G3	Tangmere Clo	23 G3	The Ridgeway	14 C5
Derwent Rd	22 B3	Maple Rd	23 E4	Taylor Clo	23 E3	Union St	14 B6
Dickens Clo	22 C4	Margaret Clo	22 C3	Telford Rd	23 G3	Water La	14 C5
Dove Grn	22 B3	Market End Way	22 C3	Thames Av	22 B4	Winters Way	14 B6
Dryden Av	22 B3	Market Sq	23 E5	The Approach	22 D3	Workhouse La	14 C5
Dumas Clo	22 B4	Mart Pl	23 G3	The Crescent	22 D4		
Dunkins Clo	22 D4	Masefield Clo	22 C3	The Oval	22 D3	**BURFORD**	
		Maud Clo	22 C3	Tinkers La	23 E5		
East St	22 D4	May Croft	23 E2	Titchener Clo	22 C3	Barn La	15 B2
Eden Way	22 B4	Medina Gdns	22 B4	Trent Cres	22 B3	Barns La	15 C3
Elm Clo	23 E2	Melville Clo	22 B4	Trinity Clo	23 E3	Cheattle Clo	15 C3
Evans Yd	23 E5	Meredith Clo	22 C3	Tubb Clo	22 C5	Cheltenham Rd	15 A3
Evenlode Clo	22 D5	Merlin Way	23 G6	Turnberry Clo	23 G3	Church La	15 C2
Ewert Clo	22 D3	Merton Walk	23 F3	Tweed Cres	22 B3	Frethern Clo	15 C3
		Meteor Clo	23 G3			Guildenford	15 C2
Fair Clo	23 E2	Middleton Stoney Rd	22 A4	Victoria Rd	23 E5	High St	15 C3
Fairford Way	23 G3	Milton Clo	22 C3	Villiers Rd	22 C5	Hunts Clo	15 B2
Fallowfields	23 F5	Murdock Rd	23 F4			Lawrence La	15 C2
Fane Clo	22 C3			Wadham Clo	23 F3	Meadow La	15 D1
Field St	22 D4	New St	23 E4	Walnut Clo	23 E2	Oxford Rd	15 C3
Filmar Ct	23 G2	North St	23 E4	Walpole Clo	22 B3	Priory La	15 B2
Finchley La	22 D5	Nuffield Clo	23 F3	Wansbeck Clo	22 B4	Pyatts La	15 C2
Fircroft	23 E1			Warwick Ct	23 G2	Sheep St	15 B2
Fleming Clo	22 C2	Oak Clo	23 E2	Waveney Clo	22 B4	Swan La	15 C2
Fox La	22 D5	Old Place Yard	23 E6	Wear Rd	22 B4	Swan Lane Clo	15 C2
		Orchard Way	22 C4	Wedgewood Rd	23 G3	Sweeps La	15 B2
Gaydon Walk	23 G2	Orwell Way	23 F3	Welland Croft	22 B4	Sylvester Clo	15 C2
George St	22 C3	Osbourne Clo	22 B4	Wellington Clo	23 F3	Tanners La	15 B2
Goldsmith Clo	22 C2	Overstrand Clo	23 F2	Wensum Cres	22 B4	Windrush Clo	15 C2
Graham Rd	22 D3	Oxford Rd	22 C6	Wesley Clo	22 C3	Witney St	15 C2
Granville Way	23 G4			West St	22 D3	Wysdom Way	15 C3
Green Clo	23 F5	Pembroke Way	23 F3	Westholm Ct	23 E5		
Greenwood Dri	22 B4	Peregrine Way	23 G6	Whitley Cres	23 F3	**CALDECOTT/**	
		Piggy La	22 D5	Willow Dri	23 E2	**SUTTON**	
Halifax Rd	23 F3	Priory Clo	23 E5	Windle Gdns	22 C4	**COURTENAY**	
Hambleside	22 B4	Priory La	23 E5	Windmill Av	23 E2	Abingdon Rd, Culham	25 H4
Hampden Clo	23 F3	Priory Rd	23 E6	Windrush Clo	22 D5	Abingdon Rd, Drayton	24 B5
Hanover Gdns	23 E5			Winterbourne Clo	22 D5	All Saints La	25 G6
Harrier Way	23 G2	Queens Av	22 D5	Winthington Rd	23 E4	Andersey Way	25 E2
Hazel Gro	23 E2			Woodfield Rd	23 E3	Appleford Rd	25 G5
Hemingway Dri	22 B4	Ray Rd	22 D5	Wordsworth Clo	22 C3	Argentan Clo	24 D2
Hendon Pl	23 F1	Raymond Rd	22 C3	Wye Clo	22 B3	Ashmole Rd	25 E2
Henley Gdns	23 E4	Reats Clo	22 C2			Bailie Clo	25 E1
Herald Way	23 G2	Redmoor Ct	22 C4	Yew Clo	23 E2	Baker Rd	25 E2
Hertford Clo	23 F4	Rochford Gdns	23 F1	York Clo	23 G3	Bergen Av	24 D2
Holly Clo	23 E2	Roman Way	23 E4			Blacknall Rd	24 D1
Hornbeam Rd	23 E1	Rookery Way	22 C4	**BLOXHAM**		Bridges Clo	24 C1
Howes La	22 A4	Rowan Rd	22 D3			Brook St	25 F6
Hudson St	22 D3	Ruck Keene Clo	22 C4	Banbury Rd	14 C5	Burton Clo	24 C1
Hunt Clo	22 D5	Ruskin Walk	23 F3	Barford Rd	14 B6	Byron Clo	24 C1
Huxley Clo	22 B4			Barley Clo	14 C5	Caldecott Clo	24 D1
		St Annes Clo	23 E3	Brickle La	14 C5	Caldecott Rd	24 D1
Ises Av	22 A4	St Anthonys Walk	23 F3	Brookside Way	14 B6	Challenor Clo	25 E2
		St Edburgs Clo	22 C5	Chapel St	14 C5	Chapel La	25 F6
Jarvis La	23 G4	St Ediths Way	22 C4	Cherrys Clo	14 B6	Chaunterell Way	24 C1
		St Hildas Clo	23 E3	Chipperfield Park La	14 C4	Church La	24 B5
Keble Rd	23 F4	St Hughs Clo	23 F3	Church St	14 B6	Church St	25 F6
Kennedy Rd	22 C4	St Johns St	23 E4	Colegrave Rd	14 C4	Churchmill Rd	25 G6
Kennet Clo	22 D5	St Marys Clo	22 C5	Colesbourne Rd	14 B6	Coleridge Dri	24 C2
Kings Av	22 D5	St Peters Cres	23 E3	Courtington La	14 B5	Corneville Rd	24 B5
Kings End	22 D5	Scampton Clo	23 G3	Cumberford	14 B5	Coromandel Clo	24 D2
Kingsclere Rd	22 C4	Scott Clo	22 C3	Cumberford Clo	14 B6	Crabtree La	24 B5
Kingsley Rd	22 C2	Severn Clo	22 B3	Gauntlets Clo	14 C4	Croasdell Clo	24 D2
Kipling Clo	22 C3	Shackleton Clo	23 G2	Greenhills Park	14 B6	Drayton East Way	24 B6
		Shakespeare Dri	22 B3	Hawke La	14 B6	Drayton Rd, Drayton	24 C6
Lambourne Cres	23 F5	Shannon Rd	22 B4	High St	14 C5	Drayton Rd, Sutton Wick	24 B4
Lancaster Clo	23 F3	Shaw Clo	22 C4	Hogg End	14 C5	Drayton Rd Ind Est	24 C1
Langford Gdns	22 C4	Sheep St	23 E4	Humber St	14 C5	Eastway	24 B6
Larch Clo	23 E2	Shelley Clo	22 C3	Kings Rd	14 B6	Ely Clo	24 C1
Launton Rd	23 E5	Skimmingdish La	23 F1	Lawrence Leys	14 C4	Ferry Walk	25 E1
Launton Rd Ind Est	23 G4	Somerville Dri	23 F3	Little Bridge Rd	14 B5	Fishermans Wharf	25 E2
Lawrence Way	22 B4	Southwold	23 E3	Little Grn	14 B6	Francis Little Dri	24 C1
Leach Rd	22 C4	Southwold La	23 E1	Merrivale La	14 C6		
Lerwick Cres	23 G2	Spenser Clo	22 C3	Old Bridge Rd	14 C5		
Lime Cres	23 E2	Spindleside	23 E2				

South Park 32 B4
Sovereign Clo 32 E3
Station Rd 32 C1
Stoner Clo 32 C1
Stonesfield 32 E3
Stour Clo 32 E2

Tamer Way 32 E2
Tavistock Av 32 B4
The Croft 32 D3
The Oval 32 A1
Thurne Vw 32 E2
Torridge Dri 32 E1
Trent Rd 32 E1

Vicarage Rd 32 D2
Viking Dri 32 F4

Wantage Rd 32 A3
Warner Cres 32 B4
Waveney Clo 32 E2
Welland Av 32 F1
Wessex Rd 32 C3
Wheatfields 32 A3
Wills Rd 32 A2
Windsor Clo 32 E3
Worcester Rd 32 F3
Wortham Rd 32 B1

Yare Clo 32 F1

EYNSHAM

Abbey Pl 33 C3
Abbey St 33 C2
Acre End St 33 B2
Back La 33 B2
Beech Rd 33 C1
Cassington Rd 33 D1
Cheltenham Rd 33 A1
Chilbridge Rd 33 A3
Clover Pl 33 B2
Conduit La 33 C2
Cuckoo La 33 A1
Duncan Clo 33 B1
Evans Clo 33 C2
Evans Rd 33 C2
Falstaff Clo 33 B2
Greens Rd 33 B1
Hanborough Clo 33 C1
Hanborough Rd 33 C1
Hawthorn Rd 33 C2
Heycroft 33 C3
High St 33 C2
John Lopes Rd 33 C2
Lombard St 33 C2
Marlborough Clo 33 C1
Marlborough Pl 33 C1
Mead La 33 D2
Merton Clo 33 B2
Mill St 33 C2
Millmoor Cres 33 C1
Newland Clo 33 C2
Newland St 33 C2
Old Whitney Rd 33 A1
Oxford Rd 33 C2
Pelican Pl 33 C1
Pinkhill La 33 B3
Queen St 33 C2
Queens Clo 33 C2
Queens La 33 C2
Shakespeare Rd 33 B1
Spareacre La 33 B1
Station Rd 33 B3
Stratford Dri 33 B1
Swan St 33 C2
Tanner La 33 C2
Thames St 33 C2
The Square 33 C2
Thornbury Clo 33 B2
Tilgarsley Rd 33 B1
Wharf Rd 33 D3
Whitney Rd 33 B1
Wytham Clo 33 C1
Wytham View 33 C1

FARINGDON

Beech Clo 33 A5
Bennett Rd 33 B4
Bromsgrove 33 B4
Butts Rd 33 B5
Canada La 33 A4
Carter Cres 33 A6
Cedar Rd 33 A4
Chestnut Av 33 A5
Church St 33 B4
Clock Tower Ct 33 A6
Coach La 33 C1
Coxwell Gdns 33 B5
Coxwell Rd 33 A6
Coxwell St 33 B5
Eagles 33 B5
Elm Rd 33 A5
Ferndale St 33 B4
Fernham Rd 33 A6
Folly View Cres 33 A6
Folly View Rd 33 A6
Gloucester Mews 33 B4
Gloucester St 33 B4
Goodlake Av 33 C1
Gravel Walk 33 B4
Hart Av 33 B4
Hawthorn Rd 33 A5
Highworth Rd 33 A5
Lansdown Rd 33 C1
Leamington Dri 33 A6
Lechlade Rd 33 A4
London St 33 B4
Maple Rd 33 A5
Marines Dri 33 B6
Market St 33 B4
Marlborough Clo 33 B5
Marlborough Gdns 33 B6
Marlborough Pl 33 A5
Marlborough St 33 B4
Orchard Hill 33 A5
Park Rd 33 B4
Portway 33 B4
Pye St 33 C1
Regal Way 33 B5
Regent Mews 33 B4
Southampton St 33 B4
Stanford Rd 33 C1
Swan La 33 B4
The Lees 33 B4
The Pines 33 A4
Town End Rd 33 B6
Untons Pl 33 C1
Westbroom 33 B4
Westland Rd 33 A5

GORING

Cleeve Down 36 D1
Cleeve Rd 36 C2
Cleve Mede 36 C1
Croft Rd 36 C3
Elm Croft 36 C3
Elmhurst Rd 36 C2
Elvendon Rd 36 C1
Fairfield Rd 36 D2
Ferne Clo 36 C2
Ferry La 36 B3
Gatehampton Rd 36 C3
Glebe Ride 36 B2
Grange Clo 36 B3
Heron Shaw 36 C2
High St 36 A2
Holmlea Rd 36 C3
Icknield Pl 36 D1
Icknield Rd 36 D1
Limetree Rd 36 C3
Little Croft Rd 36 C3
Lockstile Mead 36 C2
Lockstile Way 36 C2
Lycroft Clo 36 C2
Lyndhurst Rd 36 C2
Manor Rd 36 B3
Maple Ct 36 C2
Meadow Clo 36 C2
Mill Rd 36 C1
Milldown Av 36 C2
Milldown Rd 36 C1
Mount Field 36 C1

Nuns Acre 36 C2
Penny Piece 36 C1
Railway Cotts 36 C3
Reading Rd, Goring 36 C3
Reading Rd, Streatley 36 A3
Red Cross 36 C2
Sloane Clo 36 C2
Springfield End 36 C1
Springhill Rd 36 C1
Station Rd 36 C3
Summerfield Rise 36 D1
Thames Rd 36 B2
The Birches 36 C2
Townsend Rd 36 A1
Upper Red Cross Rd 36 C2
Valley Clo 36 C2
Wallingford Rd 36 C1
Walnut Tree Ct 36 C2
Wantage Rd 36 A1
West Way 36 C1
Whitehills Grn 36 C3
Yew Tree Ct 36 C3

GROVE/WANTAGE

Adkin Way 35 C6
Albemarle Dri 34 C3
Aldworth Av 35 E5
Alfred St 35 C7
Alfredson Pl 35 D7
Ashdown Way 34 D4
Bailey Clo 35 C5
Barbury Dri 34 C3
Barnards Way 35 E6
Barwell 35 C6
Bec Rd 35 B6
Belmont 35 C6
Blackcroft 35 C5
Blenheim Gdns 34 C3
Bosleys Orchard 34 D3
Boucher Clo 34 C3
Brereton Dri 34 C2
Bridge Farm Clo 34 D4
Broadmarsh Clo 34 C3
Brunel Cres 34 C2
Bryan Way 35 E6
Cane La 34 C4
Carlton Clo 34 C3
Catmore Clo 34 C3
Caudwell Clo 34 D3
Chain Hill 35 D7
Challow Rd 35 A7
Chandlers Clo 35 D7
Charbury Grn 34 C3
Charlton Gdns 35 E6
Charlton Pk 35 E6
Charlton Rd 35 E7
Charlton Village Rd 35 E6
Cherrytree Rd 34 E3
Church St 35 C7
Clement Clo 35 E5
Collett Way 34 C2
Collinsmith Dri 34 E2
Colne Clo 34 C3
Columbia Way 34 C3
Coopers La 35 E6
Copperfield Clo 35 C5
Cottrells Mead 34 C2
Courtenay Rd 35 D6
Cow La 34 C1
Crabhill La 34 F3
De Witre Clo 34 C3
Dean Butler Clo 35 B6
Denchworth Rd, Belmont 35 C6
Denchworth Rd, Grove 34 A1
Donnington Pl 35 C5
Easterfield 34 D2
Edington Pl 34 D3
Elizabeth Dri 35 C5
Elm Rd 35 E5
Elsworth Clo 34 D3
Euston Way 34 A3
Evenlode Clo 34 C3
Fairfield Clo 34 C3
Faraday Rd 34 A4
Farm End 34 C3

Fawley Clo 35 C5
Fetti Way 35 F6
Floral Clo 34 D3
Foliat Clo 35 E6
Foliat Dri 35 D6
Framlands Clo 35 D6
Fulmar Pl 34 C2
Fyfield Clo 35 E7
Garston Clo 35 D6
Garston La 35 D6
Gipsy La 34 E3
Glebe Gdns 34 D3
Godfreys Clo 34 E2
Gower Rd 34 A4
Grove Park Dri 34 F1
Grove Rd 35 D6
Grove St 35 C7
Ham Rd 35 B7
Hamfield 35 B7
Hampden Rd 35 D6
Hans Av 35 D6
Harcourt Grn 35 E6
Harcourt Rd 35 D6
Harcourt Way 35 D6
Hardwell Clo 34 D3
Harlington Av 34 D3
Hawksworth Clo 34 C2
Hawthorne Av 34 D3
Haywards Clo 35 D6
Highclere Gdns 35 C5
Hiskins 35 B6
Howard Av 34 E2
Humber Clo 35 D6
Hunters Clo 34 C3
Ickleton Rd 35 A7
Icknield La 35 D7
Kennett Clo 34 C3
Kingfishers 34 D3
Lark Hill 35 F7
Larkdown 35 E7
Laure Cres 34 D4
Liddiard Clo 35 D6
Limborough Hill 35 C6
Limetree Clo 34 D3
Linden Cres 34 E3
Little La 35 D6
Littleworth Hill 35 C6
Locks La 35 B7
Lydsee Gate 35 A6
Main St 34 D4
Mallard Way 34 C2
Mandarin Pl 34 C2
Mandhill Clo 34 D4
Manor Rd 35 C8
Maria Cres 35 D6
Market Pl 35 C7
Maryfield 35 D7
Mayfield Av 34 D3
Meadow Clo 34 E3
Membury Way 34 C3
Miles Dri 34 D4
Mill La 34 D4
Mill St 35 C6
Minns Rd 34 E3
Naldertown 35 B6
Newbury St 35 C7
Newlands Dri 34 C3
Nobles Clo 34 C2
North Dri 34 E2
Ogbourne Clo 35 B6
Old Mill Clo 34 D2
Orchard Way 35 D7
Ormond Rd 35 D7
Oxford La 34 D2
Paddock Clo 35 E5
Palmers 35 E6
Park Vw 35 D6
Partridge Clo 35 D7
Peregrine Way 34 C2
Port Way 35 F6
Portway 35 C7
Post Office La 35 D7
Pound Clo 34 D3
Princess Gdns 34 C3
Priory Orchard 35 B6
Priory Rd 35 C7
Roman Way 35 C5
Rosebay Cres 34 D3

St Ives La 34 D3
St Ives Rd 34 D3
St James 35 C5
St Johns Ct 34 D2
St Johns Rd 34 D2
St Marys Way 35 C6
Savile Way 34 C3
Saxon Pl 35 B6
School La 34 D2
Segsbury Rd 35 B6
Shannon Clo 34 E2
Sharland Clo 34 D4
Shepherds Clo 34 C2
Springfield Rd 35 E7
Station Rd 34 D4
Stephenson Rd 34 A3
Steptoe Clo 34 C2
Stirlings Clo 35 D6
Stirlings Rd 35 D6
Stockham Way 35 B6
Stonebury Clo 35 E6
Suzan Cres 35 D6
Swan Clo 34 C2
Teal Clo 34 C2
The Ark 35 C8
The Chestnuts 35 E6
The Kestrels 34 C2
The Maples 34 C2
The Pound 35 F6
Thornhill Clo 35 D6
Three Pigeons Clo 35 D7
Tinkerbush La 35 C6
Tirrold Way 35 E6
Trinder Rd 35 D7
Truelocks Way 35 E6
Tubbs Clo 34 C4
Tulwick La 34 E2
Upthorpe Dri 35 D6
Vale Av 34 D3
Vicarage Clo 34 D2
Wallingford St 35 D6
Wantage Bus. Pk 35 A5
Warmans Clo 35 A6
Wasborough Av 35 B6
Wayland Av 34 A4
Wayland Rd 34 C3
West Hill 35 B7
Westbrook 34 D2
Westfield Clo 34 D4
Westfield Way 35 F5
Wharf Ter 35 C6
Whitehorse Cres 34 C3
Wick Grn 34 D2
Willow La 35 C8
Willow Walk 35 D5
Wilmot Way 35 F5
Winchester Way 35 B6
Windrush Clo 34 C3
Witan Way 35 C5
Woodgate Clo 34 C3
Woodhill Dri 34 C3
Worthington Way 35 C5

HENLEY-on-THAMES

Abrahams Rd 37 C1
Adam Ct 37 D1
Adwell Sq 37 C2
Albert Rd 37 D2
Ancastle Grn 37 C2

Badgemore La 37 C1
Baronsmead 37 C1
Bell La 37 D1
Bell St 37 D1
Belle Vue Rd 37 D4
Berkshire Rd 37 C4
Blandy Rd 37 C4
Boathouse Reach 37 E2
Boston Rd 37 D3

Chalcraft Clo 37 B3
Chiltern Clo 37 A3
Church Av 37 D2
Church St 37 D2
Clarence Rd 37 C1
Clements Rd 37 B1

Coldharbour Clo 37 C4
Cooper Rd 37 C1
Crisp Rd 37 B1
Cromwell Clo 37 D4
Cromwell Rd 37 D4

Damer Gdns 37 D3
Deanfield Av 37 C2
Deanfield Rd 37 B3
Duke St 37 D2

Elizabeth Clo 37 A3
Elizabeth Rd 37 A3

Fairmile Ct 37 C1
Fairview Ind Est 37 E3
Farm Rd 37 E4
Friday St 37 D2

Gainsborough Cres 37 B3
Gainsborough Hill 37 D3
Gainsborough Rd 37 D3
Gillotts Clo 37 B4
Gillotts La 37 A4
Grange Rd 37 E3
Gravel Hill 37 C2
Gravett Clo 37 B3
Green La 37 C3
Greys Hill 37 C3
Greys Rd 37 A4
Grove Rd 37 D3

Hamilton Av 37 D3
Harcourt Clo 37 B3
Harpsden Rd 37 D4
Harpsden Way 37 D4
Hart St 37 D2
Haywards Clo 37 B3
Henley Bdge 37 D2
Hop Gdns 37 C1

King James Way 37 B3
Kings Clo 37 C2
Kings Rd 37 C1
Knappe Clo 37 B3

Lambridge La 37 B1
Lauds Rd 37 B3
Leavers Rd 37 C3
Leicester Clo 37 C1
Lovell Clo 37 B4
Luker Av 37 C1

Makins Rd 37 B4
Manor Rd 37 C4
Market Pl 37 C2
Marlow Rd 37 D1
Marmion Rd 37 E3
Matson Dri 37 E2
Meadow Rd 37 E2
Mill La 37 E4
Milton Clo 37 C2
Mount Vw 37 C1

New St 37 D1
Newtown Gdns 37 D4
Newtown Rd 37 E4
Niagara Rd 37 D4
Nicholas Rd 37 A3
Norman Av 37 D3
Northfield Clo 37 D1
Northfield End 37 C1

Orchard Clo 37 D3

Pack and Prime La 37 B2
Paradise Rd 37 B3
Park Rd 37 D3
Parkside 37 B2
Pearces Orchard 37 C1
Peppard La 37 C4
Periam Clo 37 B3
Phyllis Court Dri 37 D1
Putman Pl 37 D2

Quebec Rd 37 E3
Queens Clo 37 D2
Queens St 37 D2

Radnor Clo 37 D1
Ravenscroft Rd 37 D1
Reading Rd 37 D2
Remenham La 37 E2
River Ter 37 D2
Riverside 37 D2
Rotherfield Rd 37 D4
Rupert Clo 37 D1
Ruperts La 37 D1

St Andrews Rd 37 C4
St Annes Clo 37 C3
St Katherines Rd 37 C4
St Marks Rd 37 C3
St Marys Clo 37 A3
Sherwood Gdns 37 B3
Simmons Rd 37 C1
Singers Clo 37 D3
Singers La 37 D3
South Av 37 D4
Station Rd 37 D2

Thames Side 37 D2
The Close 37 C3
The Hocket 37 C1
Trinity Clo 37 D3
Trust Corner 37 D4
Tuns La 37 D2
Two Tree Hill 37 A3

Upton Clo 37 D3

Valley Rd 37 A3
Vicarage Rd 37 D3
Victoria Ct 37 D3

Walton Av 37 D3
War Memorial Pl 37 D4
Wargrave Rd 37 E2
Watermans Rd 37 E4
West St 37 C2
Western Av 37 D4
Western Rd 37 D3
Wharf La 37 D1
White Hill 37 F2
Wilson Av 37 D4
Wootton Rd 37 B4
Wyndale Clo 37 D3

York Rd 37 C2

HORSPATH/WHEATLEY

Acremead Rd 38 D4
Ambrose Rise 39 G4
Anson Clo 39 G4
Barlow Clo 39 E4
Beech Rd 39 F5
Bell La 39 F4
Biscoe Ct 39 G4
Blenheim La 39 E4
Blenheim Rd 38 B5
Blenheim Way 38 A5
Butts Rd 38 B6
Church Rd, Horspath 38 A6
Church Rd, Wheatley 39 F4
Collcutt Clo 38 B6
College Way 38 A6
Crown Rd 39 F4
Cuddesdon Rd 38 A6
Cullum Rd 39 G5
Elm Clo 39 G5
Elton Cres 39 G5
Farm Close La 39 F4
Farm Close Rd 39 F4
Fords Clo 38 A6
Friday La 39 F4
Gateley 38 C6
Gidley Way 38 B6
Hathaways 39 F4
High St 39 E4
Hillary Way 39 G5
Holloway Rd 39 F4
Howe Clo 39 F4
Jackies La 39 G5
Kellys Rd 38 D4
Keydale Rd 38 D4

Kiln La 39 E4
Ladder Hill 39 E6
Leyshon Rd 39 G5
Littleworth La 38 D5
London Rd 39 F4
Manor Dri 38 B6
Manor Farm Rd 38 A6
Miller Rd 39 G5
Mulberry Dri 39 F4
Old London Rd 39 G4
Old Rd 38 A3
Orchard Clo 39 F5
Oxford Rd 38 A6
Park Hill 39 F3
Roman Rd 39 G5
St Marys Clo 39 F4
Sandy La 38 B5
Simons Clo 39 F4
Spring La 38 A5
Station Rd 39 F4
Sunnyside 39 G4
Templars Clo 39 E4
The Avenue 39 G5
The Glebe 39 F4
The Triangle 39 G4
Tyndale Pl 39 G4
Westfield Rd 39 E4
Windmill La 38 D5
Wren Clo 39 F4
Wrightson Clo 38 B6

KINGSTON BAGPUIZE

Abingdon Rd 36 D5
Acacia Gdns 36 B4
Beggars La 36 A5
Bellamy Clo 36 C5
Blandy Av 36 B4
Bullockspits La 36 A6
Cherry Tree Clo 36 B5
Draycott Rd 36 B5
Faringdon Rd 36 A5
Frax Clo 36 C5
Greenheart Way 36 B5
Hanney Rd 36 B6
Harriss La 36 A4
Larch Clo 36 B4
Latton Clo 36 B5
Laurel Dri 36 B4
Lime Gro 36 B5
Norwood Av 36 C5
Oxford Rd 36 D4
Rectory La 36 D5
Rectory Lane
Trading Est 36 D6
Redwood Clo 36 B4
Rimes Clo 36 C5
Sandys La 36 B5
School La 36 C4
Spring Hill 36 A5
Stone House Clo 36 C5
Stonehill La 36 B5
Town Pond La 36 B6
Witney Rd 36 C4

LONG HANBOROUGH/FREELAND

Abelwood Rd 40 B4
Akeman St 40 A1
Beckets Way 41 B5
Blenheim La 41 B7
Boltons La 40 C3
Broad Marsh La 41 A7
Brook Way 40 B4
Chatterpie La 40 A1
Church Rd 41 C5
Church View 41B7
Churchill Way 41 B5
Clyme Way 40 B4
Evenlode Dri 40 B4
Hurdeswell 41 B5
Hurst La 41 A7
Isis Clo 41 B5

Street	Ref		Street	Ref		Street	Ref		Street	Ref
Dark La	50 D3		Weavers Clo	50 D5		Begbroke La	52 B2		Magnolia Clo	53 F4
Davenport Rd	50 C3		Welch Way	50 D4		Bellenger Way	53 E3		Manor Way	53 G1
Deer Park Rd	50 A4		Wenman Rd	50 B3		Ben Clo	53 F2		Maple Av	53 F4
Dene Rise	50 C3		West End	51 E2		Benmead Rd	53 F2		Marlborough Av	53 E1
Donnington Clo	50 B4		Westcote Clo	50 A4		Bernard Clo	52 D6		Marlborough Clo	53 E1
Dry La	50 A2		Westfield Rd	51 E2		Bicester Rd	53 G4		Marsh Clo	52 D6
Ducklington La	50 C4		Wilmot Clo	50 D5		Blandford Rd	53 E1		Mead Way	53 F1
Early Rd	51 F2		Windrush Clo	50 C3		Blenheim Rd	53 G3		Meadow View	53 F1
Eastfield Rd	51 E1		Windrush Ind Park	50 A3		Bowerman Clo	53 F3		Meadow Way	52 D6
Edington Rd	50 B3		Windrush Valley Rd	50 B3		Brandon Clo	53 E3		Merton Way	52 C6
Elm Clo	50 C4		Witan Way	51 E3		Brasenose Dri	53 G2		Mill End	53 H2
Eton Clo	51 G5		Witney Rd	50 C1		Broad Clo	53 F3		Mill St	53 G2
Fairfield Dri	50 C4		Witney Trading Est	51 E6					Morrell Clo	53 E3
Farm Mill La	51 E5		Woodgreen Hill	51 F2		Calvers Clo	53 E3		Morton Av	53 F3
Farmers Clo	51 E2		Woodlands Rd	51 F2		Cassington La	52 D6		Morton Clo	53 F3
Fieldmere Clo	50 C4		Woodstock Rd	51 F2		Cassington Rd	52 C6		Mulcaster Av	53 G3
French Clo	50 C4		Wychwood Clo	50 B3		Chamberlain Pl	53 E2		
Gloucester Pl	51 E3					Charlbury Clo	53 E1		Nurseries Rd	53 F3
Hailey Rd	51 E1		**WOODSTOCK**			Cherry Clo	53 F4		
High St	51 E4					Cherwell Av	53 G3		Oak Dri	53 G2
Highworth Pl	50 D4		Banbury Rd	48 C5		Chorefields	53 E2		Old Chapel Pl	53 G2
Holford Rd	50 C5		Bear Clo	48 C5		Church La	52 C6		Orchard Way	53 G3
Holloway Rd	50 D4		Boundary Clo	48 C5		Church St	53 G2		Oxford Rd	53 F3
Hoyle Clo	50 D1		Briar Thicket	48 C5		Churchill Rd	53 F4		
Idbury Clo	50 B4		Brook Hill	48 B5		Cleveland Clo	53 H4		Park Av	53 E1
Jacobs Clo	51 E3		Cadogan Park	48 C5		Copthorne Rd	53 F4		Partridge Pl	53 E2
Judds Clo	51 G3		Campbells Clo	48 C5		Court Clo	53 F3		Petrie Pl	53 G2
Lancut Rd	50 B3		Churchill Gate	48 C6		Croft Av	53 G3		Poplar Clo	53 G4
Lancut Rd	50 C3		Cockpit Clo	48 B5		Cromwell Way	53 G5		Pound Clo	52 C6
Langdale Gate	51 E4		Crecy Walk	48 C6		Crown Rd	53 F3		
Lowell Pl	50 D4		Farm End	48 A4		Curtis Pl	53 F2		Quarry End	52 C3
Maidley Clo	51 F2		Flemings Rd	48 D5		Curtis Rd	53 F2		Queens Av	53 H3
Manor Rd	51 F5		Glovers Clo	48 C5					Roundham Clo	53 E3
Market Sq	51 E4		Glyme Clo	48 B4		Dashwood Av	52 C6		Rowan Clo	53 F4
Marlborough La	51 E4		Green La	48 C4		Dolton La	52 A3		Rowel Dri	52 C2
Meadow View	51 F4		Harrisons La	48 B5					Rutten La	52 C5
Milking La	50 D1		Hedge End	48 C6		Edinburgh Dri	53 H3		Rutters Clo	53 E3
Mill St	51 E3		Hensington Clo	48 D5		Evans La	53 G3		
Mirfield Rd	50 C4		Hensington Rd	48 B5		Evenlode Cres	52 C1		St Johns Dri	53 G2
Moor Av	50 D3		High St	48 B5		Exeter Rd	53 F2		St Marys Clo	53 G1
Moorland Av	50 D3		Hill Rise	48 A4					St Michaels La	52 B3
Moorland Clo	50 D3		Kerwood Clo	48 C5		Fairfax Rd	53 G5		Sandhill Rd	52 C2
Moorland Rd	50 D3		Manor Clo	48 B4		Farm Clo	53 G1		Sandy La	52 C4
Mountfield Rd	50 C5		Manor Rd	48 A4		Fernhill Clo	53 E3		School Rd	53 G2
New Yatt Rd	51 E2		Market St	48 B5		Fernhill Rd	52 B3		South Av	53 G5
Newland	51 F3		Marlborough Cres	48 C5		Field Clo, Kidlington	53 G3		South Clo	53 G5
Newland Mill	51 F3		Meadow Walk	48 C5		Field Clo, Yarnton	52 C5		Spenser Av	52 C6
Newmill La	50 C1		New Rd	48 B5		Flatford Pl	53 E1		Spindlers	53 G2
Orchard Way	50 D4		Oxford Rd	48 B5		Fletcher Clo	52 C6		Spring Hill Rd	52 A3
Orkney Pl	50 D4		Oxford St	48 B5		Florence Clo	53 G3		Springfield Rd	53 G3
Oxford Hill	51 G3		Park La	48 B5		Follets Way	52 D6		Spruce Rd	53 F4
Oxlease	51 F4		Park St	48 B5		Foxglove Rd	52 C3		Sterling Clo	53 F2
Park Rd	50 C3		Parkside	48 C5		Freeborn Clo	53 G1		Sterling Rd	53 F2
Pensclose	51 F3		Plane Tree Way	48 D5		Frogwelldown La	52 A5		Stocks Tree Clo	52 C6
Pettiplace	50 C4		Princes Ride	48 C6					Stratfield Rd	53 F5
Puck La	51 E3		Recreation Rd	48 C5		Gosford Clo	53 G5		
Quarry Rd	50 D1		Rectory La	48 B5		Gravel Pits La	52 C5		The Closes	53 F2
Queen Emmas Dyke	50 D4		Rosamund Dri	48 A4		Great Close Rd	52 D6		The Garth	52 C5
Ralegh Cres	50 A4		Shipton Rd	48 C5		Green Rd	53 F3		The Hornestead	53 E3
Rissington Dri	50 B4		The Covert	48 C6		Greystones Clo	53 E2		The Moorlands	53 F1
Riverside Gdns	51 E3		The Ley	48 C5		Grovelands	53 E3		The Moors	53 E1
St Marys Mead	51 E4		Union St	48 B5					The Paddocks	52 C6
Saxon Way	50 D5		Upper Brook Hill	48 B5		Hampden Dri	53 G5		The Phelps	53 E3
Schofield Av	51 E1		Vanburgh Clo	48 B4		Hardwick Av	53 F4		The Ridings	53 E2
Schofield Gdns	51 E1		Vermont Dri	48 A4		Harts Clo	53 E3		The Rookery	53 E3
Sherbourne Rd	50 A4		Westland Way	48 A4		Hawthorn Way	53 F4		Thorne Clo	53 E2
South Lawn	50 C5					Hazel Broadway	53 G5		
Spring Clo	50 D5		**YARNTON/**			Hazel Cres	53 F5		Vicarage Rd	53 G2
Springfield Oval	50 D2		**KIDLINGTON**			Helwyns Clo	53 F1		
Springfield Pk	50 D2		Almond Av	53 F4		Heyford Mead	53 E3		Water Eaton La	53 H4
Stanton Harcourt Rd	51 G4		Andersons Clo	53 E3		High St	53 F2		Watermead	53 H2
Station La	50 D5		App Rd	53 F3		Holly Clo	53 F4		Watts Way	53 F2
Station Rd	51 E6		Asa Clo	53 G4		Home Clo	53 F2		Waverley Dri	53 G3
Swinburn Pl	50 D4		Axtel Clo	53 E2		Honor Rd	53 G3		Webbs Way	53 G2
Sycamore Clo	51 F2		Aysgarth Chase	52 C5					White Way	53 F3
Taphouse Av	51 E1		Aysgarth Rd	52 C5		Kings Way Dri	53 H3		Willow Clo	52 C5
Tarrent Av	51 G1		Azalea Av	53 G5					Willow Way	52 C2
The Crescent	51 F2					Laburnum Cres	53 F4		Wilsden Way	53 E2
The Crofts	50 D4		Banbury Rd	53 E1		Lambs Clo	53 F1		Winston Clo	53 F4
The Springs	50 D5		Barn Clo	53 E3		Lane Clo	53 E3		Wise Av	53 F2
The Willows	51 F3		Bartholomew Clo	52 C6		Langford La	52 B1		Woodstock Rd	52 A1
Thorney Leys	50 B5		Basset Way	53 G2		Lee Clo	53 E1		
Tower Hill	50 C3		Beagles Clo	53 H4		Lincraft Clo	53 F4		Yarnton La	53 E5
Vale Rd	50 C4		Beaufort Clo	53 F2		Lock Cres	53 F5		Yarnton Rd	53 F4
Valence Cres	50 B3		Beech Cres	53 F5		Lovelace Dri	53 H3		
Vanner Rd	51 F2		Begbroke Cres	52 C2		Lyne Rd	53 E2		
Viner Clo	51 F2								
Wadwards Meadow	51 F4								